MW01702241

Farmers and Figureheads

The Port of New Quay and its Hinterland

by

Sue Passmore

GHP

Grosvenor House
Publishing Limited

This book is published by
Grosvenor House Publishing Ltd
28-30 High Street, Guildford, Surrey, GU1 3EL.
www.grosvenorhousepublishing.co.uk

A CIP record for this book
is available from the British Library

ISBN 978-1-78148-509-5

To my father Dr Harry Jones (1900-1963)

CONTENTS

Acknowledgements:

I have received enormous help and encouragement from many people in New Quay and elsewhere, who willingly lent photographs and family papers and answered innumerable questions. Photographs are individually acknowledged. Sadly, since the original acknowledgements appeared, we have lost many of the older generation who were so helpful and I have amended them accordingly.

Especial thanks must go to my aunt, the late Mrs Phyllis Cosmo-Jones; my uncles, the late Captain Byron Jones, OBE and the late John Golygfor Redvers Jones; the late Mrs Mair Thomas and her sister the late Mrs Eleanor Lister; my cousin, Mrs Lilwen Lewis; the late Mr Aneurin Moller; Mrs Ruth Wood, grand-daughter of the Rev J Towyn Jones, MP; Mr Emlyn Davies, Luton, grand-son of Captain Lewis Davies, Waterloo; Mr and Mrs Martin Thomas (Phillips family papers); the late Mr Jack James, Araminta and his daughter Mrs David Highet; the late Miss Dora Evans, Montrose and her sister Mrs Melita Evans; Mrs Dorothy Harding; Mr Vivian Evans.

I am very grateful for invaluable assistance from the staffs of the following institutions: Merioneth County Library, Dolgellau; Gwynedd Archives Service; the

National Library of Wales; Ceredigion County Record Office; the National Archives, Kew; the Society of Genealogists; the Guildhall, London; the National Maritime Museum, Greenwich; the Welsh Industrial and Maritime Museum; St Fagan's Folk Museum; the Memorial University of Newfoundland; and the Maritime Museum of the Atlantic.

Quotations from Westcountrymen in Prince Edward's Isle, by Basil Greenhill and Ann Giffard; The Merchant Schooners, by Basil Greenhill; and Inshore Craft of Britain in the Days of Sail and Oar, Edgar March, are reproduced by the kind permission of their publishers, David and Charles, Newton Abbot.

Extracts from Something to Declare, Graham Smith, courtesy of Harrap. Quotations from The China Clippers are reproduced by kind permission of Brown, Son & Ferguson Ltd. I am also grateful to The Starling Press, Risca, for permission to quote from Maritime Memories of Cardiff, Captain D E Jeffreys; and to the estate of the late Alan Villiers for permission to quote from The War with Cape Horn, and to Gwynedd Archives Service for permission to quote from Growing Up Among Sailors, J Ifor Davies. I regret it has not been possible to trace the copyright holders of Puppets in Wales, by Walter Wilkinson, published by Geoffrey Bles in 1947.

This book could not have been written without the support of my children, Guy, Llywelyn and Victoria, who patiently lived with it for months and with my researches for years; with especial thanks to Guy for printing many of the photographs and for designing the cover of this new edition; to Llywelyn for checking elusive information and to Victoria for drawing the map. I am also very grateful for the constant advice and support of my much-missed sister, Angharad Rhydderch, when I was working on the first edition. Then and now, only one dedication was possible: to my father, the late Dr Harry Jones, who first encouraged my interest in local and maritime history.

Introduction:

This book is a natural development from my articles in Ceredigion, on Shipbuilding in New Quay, (1974-5), New Quay at the time of the 1851 Census, (1986); and in the Dyfed Family History Journal on Llanllwchaearn Parish in 1851, (1987). More recent research has brought into greater prominence the role of local farmers in the development of the port and in its value to the rural hinterland.* These themes are explored in Chapter I, which covers the development of New Quay as a port from the late 17th century to the early decades of the 19th century. The story is then carried through until the decline of the port with a brief look at the tourist industry as it had developed by the late 1940s. I have chosen to write about particular aspects of the development of New Quay in each chapter: the building of the pier, shipbuilding, ancillary trades and so on, rather than adhere to a purely chronological approach as this retains all the appropriate information in an easily consulted format. However the later chapters take us nearer the inevitable end to a great era in the history of not only one small port but also the maritime history of

* I would recommend also my Llanllwchaearn: a parish history (2010), my article on investing in shipping in Dyfed FHS, (2011) and Llanina & Cytblwyf (2011).

Britain, in which New Quay played a vital role. The penultimate chapter relates details of New Quay's coasting and deep-water vessels and the men who manned them, for their story was to continue into the twentieth century, long after New Quay's own ships were firewood.

Many links with the past have vanished with the long passage of time, perhaps the greatest vandalism was the destruction of the limekiln on Traeth-y-Dolau to create the Tourist Office! In the first edition of this book I expressed the hope that a Maritime Museum would be created here and this wish has now been fulfilled, with the excellent little Heritage Centre on the pier, so valuable in giving each new generation an awareness of their past. It is also much appreciated by visitors.

As almost twenty years has elapsed since this book first appeared it has had to be updated, and new material has been included. The opportunity was also taken to correct minor errors which occurred in the first edition.

List of Plates

Chapter I

Farmers and Figureheads

The village of New Quay, as we see it today, grew up almost wholly in the 19th century. However, its growth was set in motion by market forces in the last quarter of the 17th century. That was a time of general increase in wealth after the restoration of Charles II and more money was available for investment. The ripples of this development were felt in the remote parish of Llanllwchaearn, then inhabited, according to the Hearth Tax returns of 1670, by some 51 households. Only 17 householders could afford to pay tax for their hearths and these were the farmers and craftsmen. Some of the farms appear on a survey of 1587, like Cefn Gwyddil and Crawgal, and descending in their respective owners' families until the 19th century. Others certainly date from the early part of the 17th century at least, such as Penrhiw Pistyll, inhabited by David ap Jenkin in the mid 17th century and still being farmed by his descendants over a hundred years later. It was not sold away from the family until 1831. This security of possession must have contributed to the farmers' ability to invest in ships and to build a "new key" to protect their investments in the 1690s.

This new quay still stands today, though it has long been overshadowed by the more impressive pier built in the 19th century. The original quay was stoutly, if crudely, constructed of massive boulders and stakes and is known as Penpolion. It was reinforced with concrete in the 1950s but was certainly sufficient in the 17th and 18th centuries to shelter the small, usually ten ton cargo vessels then being purchased, probably from Cardigan. Cardigan was the Deputy Port for Milford Haven, with particular responsibility over the area from Fishguard to Aberaeron; a system set up in the 16th century. It was natural, therefore, that local entrepreneurs should look to Cardigan for guidance in their new venture.

The earliest New Quay vessel known so far, was the Speedwell, master Evan John, which appears in the Port Book of Cardigan in 1698. (1) In March 1700, Jenkin David purchased the Catherine, of which he was master, carrying cargoes for himself and not for Cardigan merchants as the other New Quay vessels did: the Saviour, Arthur, Maria and Hopewell. Jenkin David may have been a son of Penrhiw Pistyll farm and the new vessel was perhaps named for his mother, Catherine. The arrival of the vessel was of such significance to the area that no fewer than four girls were christened Catherine that month to mark the occasion. From these small beginnings grew the carrying trade which was the main task of New Quay ships for the next two hundred years. The area produced nothing that was exportable, except perhaps some farm produce, but there was plenty of money to be earned carrying grain from Cardigan to Barmouth or Pwllheli, and bar-iron to Pwllheli or Caernarfon or culm (small coal) from half a dozen

Pembrokeshire ports to Cardigan or New Quay. References to sailors were already appearing in the 17th century Bishops' Transcripts and make it clear that the vessels were manned by local men.

Salt was a valuable cargo too - just how valuable one learns from a smuggling affray which took place here on the night of 5th/6th August, 1704. A Salt Duty had first been imposed in 1643, but withdrawn, because of its unpopularity, by Charles II, in the wave of euphoria which followed his return from exile in 1660. It was nowhere more unpopular than on this coast where the seasonal herring fishing had been an important part of the local economy since at least the 16th century. Salted herrings and salt meat were important items in the winter diet of the people and the re-imposition of the duty in 1694, by William and Mary, meant that it was well worth smuggling in salt from Ireland. The strength of the smuggling organisation was discovered the hard way by John Bevan, a riding officer of Tywyn, Merionethshire, when, following a tip-off, he and his seven men pursued several barques along the coast until they attempted to land their illegal cargo of salt at New Quay. There Bevan was confronted by a crowd which he estimated was 150 strong, with 200 horses to carry away the salt. The Revenue men had simply no chance and when they were forced to fire on the crowd to protect themselves, as he subsequently informed his bosses at the Salt Office in London, they were arrested by the local constables and one of his men, Remarke Bunwoith, who had seriously wounded a smuggler, was bound over to appear at the Sessions. (2) The Salt Office cannot have been too pleased at the obvious sympathy of the local

Justice of the Peace, Captain Lewis, with the smugglers, but such was the case and smugglers even took orders from the gentry for silk and candles. (3) Both the legal and the illegal trade in salt continued throughout the 18th century. The names of few vessels have survived but there is a reference to the Hopeful of New Quay, master Griffith David, in the Quarter Sessions records of 1745 (4), when he testified that while bringing his cargo of salt from John Blackburn's works at Liverpool the previous autumn, because of storms part of the cargo had been lost and he appealed for the remittance of duty which had been paid on it. Folk memory too has preserved the exploits of Sion Cwilt, New Quay's most famous 18th century smuggler, who was responsible for the distribution of smuggled goods. He lived in a cottage on the moorland above Synod Inn, still known as Banc Sion Cwilt today, and derived his name from his patchwork coat. He appears as John Qwilt in the parish registers of Llannarth, when his grandson was baptised there in 1758; and he was still living in 1771 when his wife was buried there. Among the smugglers' opponents were Richard Phillips, who was a Salt Officer at New Quay for many years, he was buried at Llanllwchaearn in 1813, aged 85; John Davies, tidewaiter, whose task was to board ships entering port and enforce proper observation of the customs regulations; and in the last decades of the 18th century New Quay had her own Riding Officer, Joseph Jones (1759-1839). His great-great-great-great-great grandson, Noel Davies, recalled in his autobiography (5) that he was told in his childhood, by elderly relatives, of Joseph patrolling the coast with 17 armed men to stop the smuggling of salt.

Despite the regular trade in salt and other cargoes as we have seen, Lewis Morris of Anglesey, the famous man of letters and cartographer, did not feel it was necessary to provide a plan of the approaches to New Quay in his Plans of the harbours, Bays, Bars and Roads in St George's Channel, produced in 1748, and only mentions the place in passing as 'a resort of small fishing vessels'. There were certainly excellent herring catches at this period. The herring came inshore in the autumn as they do today, so that nets are frequently set just off the beach at New Quay. It is probable that men who were agricultural labourers at other seasons of the year, turned fishermen in the herring season. (6) The price of a boat might well have been beyond the average fisherman at this period and it appears that local farmers leased them out. Some evidence of this practice comes from the will of William Jones, gentleman, of Fforch-cwm (near Cross Inn), who died in 1786. Apart from his land, he bequeathed his 'fishing boat and all its appurtenances with all my nets to my said wife Jane and son William jointly', provided that Jane was agreeable, otherwise William is to have only three of the nets. The inventory taken at the time of his death valued the fishing boat and nets at £7/7/-, a considerable proportion of his goods and chattels whose total amounted to only £19/9/-.

In the 1940s, a description of the traditional way of dividing the herring catches was given by Phil Jones of New Quay to Griffith Jenkins, Arfon View, and deposited at the National Library of Wales. (7) "In a sailing vessel, every 7th herring to the boat, or if a rowing boat, every 9th herring; of the remainder half went to the crew and half to the nets". This confirms that fishermen did not always own their own boats or even the nets, since their share was allocated separately. Hence the significance of leaving the nets separately to William the younger, who would have been entitled to the catch on three nets only, while his mother received the herrings allocated to the owner of the boat and to the remaining nets.

In the last quarter of the 18th century, a new venture was set afoot: shipbuilding began in New Quay. Shipbuilders were hired in Aberystwyth: such as David Peter, father of the future Rev. David Peter, who came here in 1772 to set up a yard, although the first vessel known to have been built here was the Thomas and Mary, launched in 1779. She was a 24 ton sloop, single-masted and fore-and-aft rigged as all her smaller predecessors probably were. From now onwards the progress of New Quay was part and parcel of the 18th century revolutions in agriculture and industry. Prys Morgan, in The Eighteenth Century Renaissance in Wales, takes as his theme the revival of Wales from a period of stagnation and speaks of the proliferation of societies aimed at "improvement" which were a characteristic of the age. Their leading lights were frequently, though not always, the gentry, and New Quay's leading landowners were no exception. Naturally they were interested in any development which increased the value of their property although they were also philanthropically inclined as well. To such men the potential for development in New Quay seemed limitless. In 1794, the Rev Lewis Turnor of Wervil Brook, a farm on the Cardigan Road, wrote a book entitled General View of the Agriculture in Cardiganshire, with Mr T Lloyd. He had made his own

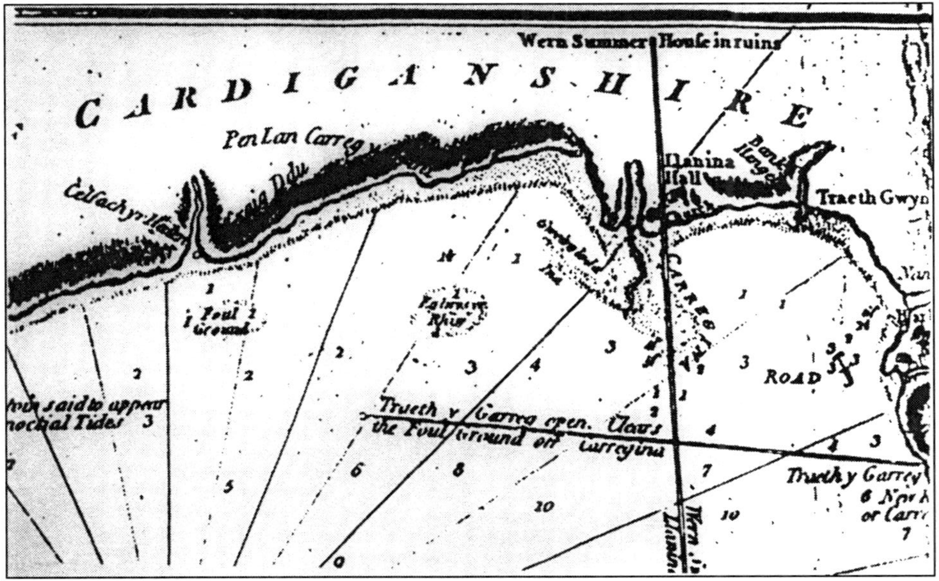

The sea approach to New Quay from William Morris' s plan, dated 1801. Note the original name: Traeth Gwynne. This commemorates the seventeenth century owners of Llanina mansion, the Gwynnes of Llanrhystud. Nant Gwynne marks the boundary of their property.

farm a model of efficiency by the standards of the day and was interested in increasing the market for his produce. He envisaged New Quay as an ideal site for a packet station to Ireland, emphasising that the distance from London to New Quay was less than that to either Holyhead or Milford, which at that time were the only places offering direct communication with Ireland. His book reinforced the already strong interest in the development of the port. As a result of the Industrial Revolution there was an increasing demand for small sailing ships to carry cargoes around the coast of Britain and Europe and also on deep water, to North and South America and even Australia. The increasing importance of New Quay as a centre of maritime activity is shown by the fact that William Morris, Lewis's son, when producing a new edition of his father's great work, mentioned above, in 1801, included a plan of the approaches to the port, proving that the intervening half-century had greatly increased its significance.

The modern history of New Quay may be said to have begun with the purchase by John Evans, husbandman of Llanychaearn, and Lewis Lewis, innkeeper of Newcastle Emlyn, of the estate of "Noyadd y Towyn, Ty'r Eglwys or Ty'r Plas" in 1791 for £900, from Thomas Jones of Coedstre, Carmarthenshire. John Evans had already been investing in local shipping even before he purchased the estate. He commissioned the sloop Peggy and Betsey, built at New Quay in 1787. An increasingly important cargo was limestone, necessary to improve the acid land of the county at four tons an acre; lime kilns were built at Cei Bach, Traethgwyn and New Quay. Another early investor was Evan Phillip, Penrhyn, yeoman, who owned shares in the 58 ton Speedwell, launched in 1804. John Jordan Jones, Esq of Fronwen, Llannarth, had 32 shares in the sloop Elinor, built in New Quay in 1802; he already owned the Betsey, built at Cardigan in 1792. William Jones, who farmed Cefn Coed Isaf, had 21 shares in the Royal Oak, launched in 1810; Thomas Jones, gentleman, of Pantclynhir farm, had 16 shares in the 31 ton sloop Friendship, launched in 1810 and a similar investment in the smaller Delight, built in 1814. John Owen of Ciliau, a farm of over 250 acres in Llandysuliogogo, was another lifelong investor in New Quay ships, as was his son in the second half of the 19th century. James Jones, Pendderw, another Llandysuliogogo farmer, had shares in the Eagle in 1808 and invested in ships for the next twenty-odd years. (8) The Longcrofts of Llanina, who inherited the estate after the death of Edward Warren Jones in 1829, were to be closely involved with the building of the new pier, together with the descendants of John Evans, Llanychaearn. These and others like them were the men in whose hands the future of New Quay lay; they owned the land on which the village would be extended; they would lease sites for smithies, shipyards, public-houses, chapels, schools and cottages. Prosperity beckoned not only for those already wealthy; the booming port also offered a focus for the ambition of the poor in its rural hinterland and many a landless youth made his way to New Quay, so that the next generation might become "upwardly mobile" and fill the ranks of its innumerable Master Mariners as well as much-needed craftsmen. The stage was set for the "economic miracle"(9) of the 19th century.

At the time of John Evans' and Lewis Lewis' purchase, there were only three houses and six cottages on their

1200 acres property. These three houses were probably Neuadd farm, Towyn and Pen-y-wig. All three remain today, although only Neuadd is still a working farm. Pen-y-wig, sited above the foreshore, is now much altered and its farm land built over: the Blue Bell Inn for example stands where its out-houses once acted as a wind-break, people still alive when I was collecting the information for this book, could remember cows grazing on the slope which rises behind it. The six cottages would have included those at Porth-yr-Eglwys - today known as Rectory Square, in one of which lived John-y-Clochy, John the bell ringer, who was also the sexton, in the 18th century. Also possibly the cottages known as Winllan, on the lane which ran from the churchyard through Neuadd woods, and once led to a ropeyard behind Lewis Terrace, which remained in occupation until the council houses were built in the 1940s; the pair of cottages near Towyn (which probably counted as one, since most cottages were built in pairs) and the Dolau Inn.

Another early building on the waterfront, adjacent to Pen-y-wig farm, was the Efail fawr, the big smithy, and this may well date from the 17th century, as several smiths are named in the Hearth Tax returns and the Bishops' Transcripts. In 1802 the Efail fawr was occupied by David John David and his sons and grandson would operate it until the latter's death in 1896. The "Gofion", blacksmiths, and their connections, formed one of New Quay's "tribes" as the descendants of the oldest families were known.

What else would you have observed if you were able to go back in time and walk about New Quay in 1810, when the port was beginning to grow? First, one would

New Quay 1890

be struck by the absence of the pier, so familiar a part of the New Quay scene today - it was not built until 1835; secondly the brand-new Revenue Watch-house on the bluff between Dolau Beach and Pen-y-wig reef on which the pier would be built. (Today the Revenue Watch-house and the Efail Fawr opposite are both restaurants.) Along the seafront from Pen-y-wig were a few new little clom-walled thatched cottages. Clom is the Welsh equivalent of cob: the walls are built up of layers of mud and chopped straw which are allowed to dry level by level, lime washed and then topped with a thatched roof, done in a very distinctive design in this area. The style was both durable and weatherproof and it is a great loss that none of New Quay's clom cottages now remain; the last was torn down about forty years ago. Beyond the cottages was a simple white-washed square stone building, the new Tabernacle Methodist Chapel, standing half-way up the hill between Pen-y-wig and the Black Lion Inn, which stood on land belonging to the Llanina Estate. Older cottages stood on the foreshore itself where the Watersports Centre keeps its boats today.

This photograph taken about 1890 gives an excellent indication of how New Quay developed over the years and also shows some vanished features of the village. Still on the Front, stand thatched roof examples of early cottages, probably built after 1790. Next to them centre left is the large white building of Tabernacle Chapel built in 1807. Across the road from the chapel is the now vanished smithy of Griffith Griffith and below is the neat white-washed building which was once a public house, known as the Blue Lion, where a murderous quarrel broke out in 1776 resulting in the death of David

Ephraim. It has now been replaced by modern houses. On the beach itself, where the lifeboat house now stands, the pine end of a house is visible. The houses built here, among the earliest in the village, were known as Tangeulan or "the Downs". The stone storehouse, below the clom cottages, was erected about 1775. High Terrace had been begun behind the Front by the 1840s and Picton Terrace was built behind that in the 1870s. Cows from Penwig farm which still stood, just out of frame on the right of the picture, grazed the grassy hill behind the modern buildings. The larger vessels in the harbour include smacks and a ketch.

The Revenue Watch-house had been considered a necessity because smuggling still played an important part in the secret economy of the area, although it was of less significance as the local prosperity increased. The duty on salt would remain in force until 1825 and it continued to be smuggled along with soap, candles and whisky. To the Riding officers, who had patrolled the coast since their institution in 1698, was now added "a preventive Water Guard, established in 1809, to link up with the other services. The coast was divided into three: Carlisle to Land's End; Land's End to the North Foreland and North Foreland to Berwick. Naval Officers were appointed and given the title of 'Inspecting Captains'. They were to sail up and down the coasts of their divisions and to check on the cruisers and boats under their command. There were ten cruisers and thirteen boats on the Western coast .... There was thus a triple cordon around the coasts which the smugglers would have to penetrate - the Revenue cruisers out at sea, the Preventive Water Guard in coastal waters and the Riding

Officers... Although not at first highly regarded, the Preventive Water Guard became an effective force in combating smuggling and was the immediate ancestor of HM Coastguard" (10).

When the Napoleonic Wars came to an end with the Battle of Waterloo in 1815, many demobilised sailors were recruited to strengthen the Water Guard as the Government was afraid they might be tempted to use their skills in smuggling. Boatmen had to be between the ages of 20 and 35, with six years service at sea or seven if they were fishermen. Each station had a Chief Officer, generally a naval lieutenant, a Chief Boatman, two Commissioned Boatmen and four Boatmen. They had a four-oared gig or six-oared galley, for use along the coast and the Riding officers continued to be employed to patrol inland. On 15th January 1822 the now familiar name "Coastguard" was officially employed for the Preventive Water Guard, Cruisers and Riding Officers.

"They came on duty at dusk and went to bed at dawn. Every night they were assembled in the watch room, armed with pistol and cutlass or with musket and bayonet... no man was given his instructions until he reported for duty and he was forbidden to communicate with his family after he received them... the guard was inspected twice a night to see if it was alert and watchful."(11) Besides a room for mustering the men, the Revenue Watch-house at New Quay also provided living accommodation for the Chief Officer and his family.

As had been the policy for years with the Riding Officers and Customs men, the coastguards were not local men, to avoid the risk of collusion and they were frequently moved around so that they would not become too friendly with the local population. The earliest list of coastguards posted to New Quay, dating from 1826 (in the National Archives at Kew), shows that most of the coastguards came from the southern counties of England and one from Tenby. Some also came from Ireland. The first Chief Officer under the new system was Joshua Wortley from Elmer, Kent and in 1828 he changed places with Jonathan Webb from Portreath. Charles Childs, who came as a Boatman in 1826 from Tenby, moved on to Southampton in 1832. Houses were generally rented for them and their families in the village. As the years passed and smuggling was in decline, many of the boatmen remained at their posts for ten or fifteen years, like John Noall from Portland, Dorset, who was first posted to New Quay in 1830 and remained there until he retired in 1845. Boatmen and Commissioned Boatmen retired at 50, Chief Boatmen at 55 and Chief Officers at 60. A number chose to remain in New Quay on their retirement, like John Mears, also from Portland, who was first posted to New Quay in 1846 and lived in Mason Row, later Mason Square. His wife Harriet was from Chichester in Sussex and their four sons were born in Dorset and Sussex. John died in New Quay in 1886 aged 76 and his son John Duke Mears became a grocer here. Another who settled in New Quay and was a staunch supporter of Tabernacle Sunday School was George John, who lived at 18 Church Street and married a woman from Llandysul when his first wife died.

When the Coastguards were reorganised, they were given responsibility for life-saving as well as tracking down smugglers and were issued with "Manby's Mortar", which had been tested and officially approved by the Board of Ordnance. Each station was supplied with one and every member of the crew was instructed in its use. It was the invention of Captain Manby, a boyhood friend of Lord Nelson. Basically it consisted of firing a shot with a line attached from the shore to the wrecked ship. It was a device which was to save many lives before the rocket was developed. A Lifeboat would not be stationed in New Quay until 1864. If the Mortar was already available in New Quay in 1814, it may have been used to save the crew of the 200 ton Helen, Captain Fitzgerald, which became a total loss. In 1816, the 200 ton Ellipse, Captain Qualdro, was wrecked here and the inhabitants of New Quay saved the crew. In the same year the Mary Fell, 200 tons, under the command of Captain Wallace, was also wrecked in the bay; and so was the 400 ton Venerable, bound for Liverpool in 1818.

Inevitably the local people benefited from shipwrecks, if they could elude the sharp eyes of authority. There are many stories of wreckers on this coast, as in other areas of the British Isles, stories of misleading lights designed to lure ships to their doom. Howell Harris, the Methodist leader, visiting nearby Penbryn parish in the 1740s, felt it necessary to preach sermons against the practice of cheating the Government of excise duties and the cruel treatment of shipwrecked sailors. He is said to have been preaching to a crowd at Neuadd farm when his audience unaccountably began drifting away; some late arrival had reported a ship being driven ashore and, according to the story, he soon had no-one left to hear him. However there is simply no mention of this incident in his diaries, although he certainly took a close interest in the fledgling Methodist circuit he had organised in this area. Salvaging goods from wrecks remained popular especially at times of great poverty in Cardiganshire and David Davies, Moylon Farm, (12) Troed-yr-aur, reported on 28th December 1816, to his son, Dr Daniel Owen Davies, who had served in the Peninsular War with the Duke of Wellington and had not yet returned home: "A French brig was wrecked with a cargo of wines on Penbryn Sands this day fortnight, which I am sorry to relate to the disgrace of my countrymen, who drank too hearty of the wine that seven of 'em died and many more would if it were not for the timely assistance of doctors."(13).

Howell Harris's little band of disciples in the area met at Coed-y-brain. On 20th June 1744, William Richard, who was responsible for the Methodists in the Diocese of St David's up to Aberaeron, visited Coed-y-brain and reported: "They are but young Christians without it being two or three and they are very plain in their experience!... I doubt not but the lord has visited several of them effectually."(14) Howell Harris himself wrote constantly about the "Lambs" in Wales. But his influence here dwindled after 1752 when he became more engrossed in his militia force during the Seven years' War (1756-1763) and with building up his community at Trevecca and it was his former friend, the Rev Daniel Rowland of Llangeitho and the latter's protégé Thomas Grey (1733-1810), who subsequently had the most influence in developing the Methodist cause here. Grey was born at Llangyfelach and worked first as a collier; through grants from the Congregational

Fund he was educated at the Academy at Abergavenny and became pastor of the Independent churches at Llwynpiod and Abermeurig, Cardiganshire in 1762. Working closely with Daniel Rowland, he established branches at New Quay, Llannarth, Ffos-y-ffin and Llanddewi Aberarth. He was described as a man of great stature, rough mien and a majestic figure in his large puritan wig. His adherents were accustomed to walk to Ffos-y-ffin for communion. Preaching meetings at New Quay took place at the house of John Owen. When Evan Evans' John Evans' son came to occupy Pen-y-wig in 1802, the cause was given a fillip and henceforth adherents met at Pen-y-wig. According to the Hanes Methodistiaid Rhan Ddeheuol Aberteifi Mr Evans gave the land on which Tabernacle was built.

The local Methodist organiser at this time was Mr Ebenezer Morris, then based at Pensarn Chapel and he was reluctant to found another new chapel. However Evan Evans' wife Catherine and Mrs Catherine Parry of Byrlip farm, New Quay, went to see him and persuaded him to allow them to erect a chapel on the land her husband was willing to give. Mr Morris was won over but made it a condition that he chose the site and it is an impressive one. Before the present houses were built on Pengeulan, the chapel dominated the cottages and as late as the early 1900s was clearly visible from all parts of the Front. It was built in 1807. No permanent preacher was, however, appointed, even though in 1811 the Calvinistic Methodist position was regularised and they were ordaining their own preachers for their societies, according to a form drawn up rather reluctantly by the Rev Thomas Charles of Bala, himself ordained in the

Anglican church. Some of the more conservative Methodist societies were reluctant to receive the sacrament at the hands of these Methodist ministers. But the break with the established church was complete. It appears that it was not until the 1840s that Tabernacle had a permanent minister: the Rev Evan Jones from Llangeitho. Among the early trustees of the chapel were Evan Evans, Penwig,; Thomas Parry, "Purlip", who knew his Bible well though unable to write; John Owen; John Thomas Owen, who was fond of stopping people on the road and asking them about their immortal souls; Thomas Morgan the butcher; Solomon Williams, Coastguard; William Davies, Coastguard, from Milford; Thomas Davies, Traethgwyn; Evan Timothy, merchant, his son David and his grandson, William, a Justice of the Peace. It was a far cry from the days when the young society met at Coed-y-brain, unobtrusively, for fear of persecution.

At this time New Quay's Independents or Congregationalists still worshipped at Penrhiwgaled Chapel near Cross Inn, built in 1783, but by 1828 they were sufficiently numerous to build their own chapel at Maen-y-groes, nearer and more convenient to attend, reached by the old road up Cwm Gido. Among the founders were Thomas Thomas who farmed Cefn Gwyddil, Joseph Davies, Carn-y-geifr, David Thomas, who lived on Gwaun-yr-efail land, David Evans, carpenter, New Quay, William Evans, Pencnwc and Thomas Richards, Bwlch-cefn. It was erected under the supervision of Mr Daniel Thomas, who had come to Penrhiwgaled as minister in 1818. He was the son of Dafydd Thomas of Llanbedr Felfre in Pembrokeshire and was born in 1785. He was a very successful preacher and 160 new members were recorded in 1822. He married Mrs Rachel Thomas, widow of Abraham Thomas, Llwyn-onn farm, Llanina and took a great interest in all local matters, investing in ships and becoming a director of the Harbour Company, before his death in 1848. (15)

Just below Tabernacle Chapel, perched on a shelf of land halfway down the cliff, was a small cottage public-house, which had stood there since the late 18th century at least. It was then known as the New Storehouse, named for the large stone warehouse nearby, built to accommodate goods landed at Penpolion. The warehouse now houses the Marine Centre. By the 19th century the little pub had changed its name to the Blue Lion, generally known as the Blue, perhaps because the earlier name was associated with a tragic incident: a quarrel between a drunken tinker and a fisherman, which culminated in the latter's murder at Penpolion in 1776. The Quarter Sessions records recount the fate of David Ephraim, son of Ephraim Samuel, a longtime inhabitant of the area, who had married in Llanllwchaearn church fifty years before and had ten children, of whom David was the youngest but one, baptised 20th February 1747. David shared his boat with David Evans, Llandysuliogogo and in the early hours of the morning of 14th June 1776 they were making their way down to Penpolion when they decided to stop at the pub for a drink. There were a number of late carousers there, including Edward Jones, a tinker, from Llangoedmor. An argument developed over the drinks and when David Evans and David Ephraim left, Edward Jones and his friends followed them and the argument was renewed at Penpolion. Jones seized a soldering iron and struck David Ephraim several times on the head, inflicting a fatal wound: Ephraim collapsed into the boat and died. Edward Jones was found guilty of manslaughter. His victim's burial is recorded in the Parish register as a "cruel death" and he was provided with a wooden coffin. The average person was then still buried simply in a woollen winding sheet, in obedience to the 1667 and 1678 laws passed to encourage the woollen trade.(16)

Below the "Blue", there were cottages along the beach known variously as Tangeulan, the "Downs" or Windsor Terrace; and as mentioned earlier, cottages along Traeth-gwyn and Cei Bach, where there was also a stone quay like Penpolion, of which only the shingle foundation remains. Such sites between the cliff and the spring flood tide had been very popular for centuries as the ownership of such ground was often uncertain or common and there were no rates to pay. Many of the cottages along Traeth-gwyn beach have also long gone as a result of erosion, almost within living memory fields were being harvested there which have now crumbled into the sand. There were once cottages on Dolau Beach adjacent to the limekiln, which was only destroyed a few years ago when the Tourist Information Centre was built above the beach and the access to the beach was widened. The river valley of Cwm Gido which flowed down to Traeth-gwyn and belonged to Edward Warren Jones of Llanina, also had a cluster of cottages and there were more on Penrhiw Pistyll land around Glyngolau farm and its malt-house. At this time a number of shipyards were already operating along the beaches, but their activities will be discussed fully in Chapter III.

Information about the careers of New Quay sailors at this time is to be found in the Trinity House Petitions, which are of enormous interest to the maritime historian and the genealogist, since the petitioners give a resume of their careers at sea and details of their dependents. For centuries, the ancient corporation of Trinity House, by virtue of its charter granted in 1514, had been concerned with distributing charitable funds for the benefit of poor disabled seamen, their widows and orphans. Unfortunately, because of the Great Fire of London in 1666, another fire in 1714 and enemy action in 1940, comparatively few records of these charitable disbursements have survived. However, there are still a considerable number available for the period 1787-1854 when the passing of the Mercantile Act brought this part of their duties to an end. (17)

Evan Evans of New Quay recorded in his petition that he first went to sea at the age of 15 in 1799 on board the Nancy, a sloop of 163 tons built in Devon in 1792 and employed in the coasting trade. The following year he served in the 25 ton sloop Seahorse. By 1801 he was mate aboard the 40 ton sloop Betsey, built in Cardigan in 1797, and owned, like the Nancy, in New Quay. The break-down of the Peace of Amiens in May 1803 meant that there was an increased demand for sailors to man the Navy's ships in the Napoleonic Wars. To this day, the menace of the press-gang remains in folk-memory in New Quay with recollections of various subterfuges employed by ancestors to escape its clutches. A regular feature of merchant ships' expenses was the payment of protection money against the impressments of members of the crew, ranging from 2/6 to 11/6 depending on status: whether boy or mate. Whether Evan Evans was

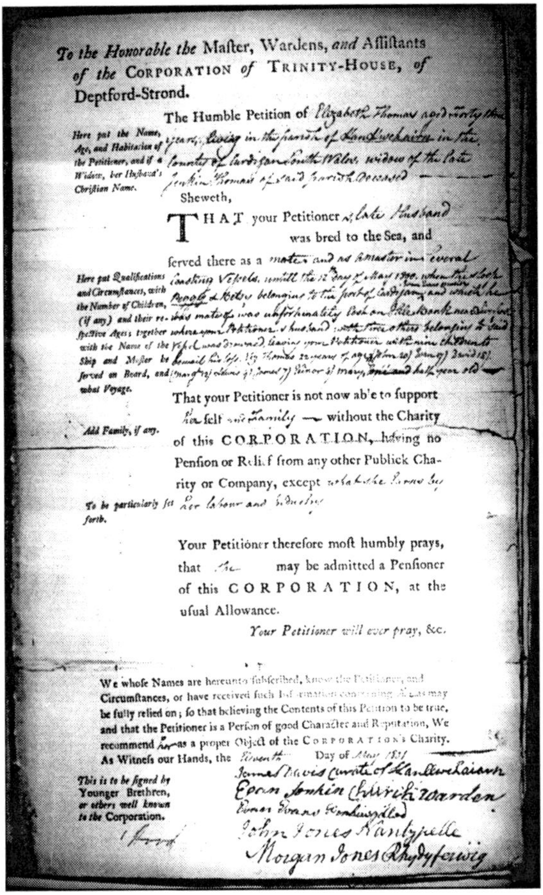

To the Honorable the Master, Wardens, *and* Assistants *of the* CORPORATION *of* TRINITY-HOUSE, *of* Deptford-Strond.

The Humble Petition of Elizabeth Thomas aged forty three years, living in the parish of Llandewchaiarn in the County of Cardigan South Wales, widow of the late Jenkin Thomas of said parish deceased

Here put the Name, Age, and Habitation of the Petitioner, and if a Widow, her Husband's Christian Name.

Sheweth,

THAT your Petitioner's late Husband was bred to the Sea, and served there as a mate and as master in several Coasting Vessels, untill the 12 day of May 1800, when the sloop Peggy & Betsy belonging to the port of Cardigan and which he was mate of was unfortunately lost on Hile Bank near Liverpool whereupon Petitioner's husband with three others belonging to said Vessel was drowned, leaving your Petitioner with nine children to bewail his loss. [illegible]

Here put Qualifications and Circumstances, with the Number of Children, (if any) and their respective Ages; together with the Name of the Ship and Master he served on Board, and what Voyage.

That your Petitioner is not now able to support herself and family without the Charity of this CORPORATION, having no Pension or Relief from any other Publick Charity or Company, except what the Parish [illegible] her labour and Industry

Add Family, if any.

To be particularly set forth.

Your Petitioner therefore most humbly prays, that she may be admitted a Pensioner of this CORPORATION, at the usual Allowance.

Your Petitioner will ever pray, &c.

We whose Names are hereunto subscribed, know the Petitioner, and Circumstances, or have received such Information concerning [illegible] may be fully relied on; so that believing the Contents of this Petition to be true, and that the Petitioner is a Person of good Character and Reputation, We recommend her as a proper Object of the CORPORATION'S Charity.

As Witness our Hands, the Eleventh Day of May 1801

This is to be signed by Younger Brethren, or others well known to the Corporation.

James Davis Curate of Llanllwchaiarn
Evan Jenkin Churchwarden
Evan Evans [illegible]
John Jones Nantypelle
Morgan Jones Rhydyfenwig

Trinity House Petition. Courtesy of the Society of Genealogists. This petition was presented in 1801 by Mrs Elizabeth Thomas of New Quay. She was then 43, the widow of Jenkin Thomas, "who had served as mate and as master in several coasting vessels, until the 12th day of May 1800 when the sloop Peggy & Betsey (owned by John Evans, Pen-y-wig and Towyn), master Evan Evans, was unfortunately lost on Hile bank (sic) Liverpool, leaving your Petitioner with nine children to bewail his loss". The children's names and ages are listed.

press ganged or not the Petition does not relate, but it seems more likely that he volunteered to serve in the Navy as he states that he was a Petty Officer in 1807 aboard HMS Delight. He saw service in the Mediterranean and was still in the Navy in 1812, on HMS Le President, captured from the French. He left the Navy when the war ended in 1814 and bought himself a small sloop which he named Delight after his wartime posting and returned to the coasting trade, voyaging between New Quay, Bristol and Liverpool. When he put in his petition he was crippled with rheumatism but still limped to church proudly wearing his medal (belatedly awarded in 1847 like all the rest for those who served in that then long ago war) on his clean but shabby coat, as his sponsor, the Officer Commanding Coastguard, Joseph Barrett, described in his eloquent plea for assistance in this deserving case.

Another petition details the career of Owen Davies of New Quay, who first went to sea in 1798 at the age of 14. His first vessel was the Seahorse, mentioned above, and he continued in coasting vessels until 1806 when he was an Ordinary Seaman on the Neptune trading to the West Indies. This demonstrates an early connection between the port and deep-water or Foreign trade, as opposed to the Home Trade which encompassed the British Isles and Northern Europe. The Napoleonic Wars added a new hazard to the more usual ones of wind and weather: privateers. These were sea-raiders issued with a licence to prey on the enemy's vessels in wartime and their threat was often close to home. For instance, the sloop Hope, of Cardigan, was captured by the Bohemienne in the first week of November 1807, although at that date the Irish sea was quite well protected by British warships. Certainly a good deal better than it had been a few years earlier during the American War of Independence when John Paul Jones, the American privateer, and his French allies had sailed these seas almost with impunity and captured several Welsh vessels. At least four Barmouth vessels were taken in the 1780s and their crews sent to languish in French gaols, till they could be ransomed, which often took years of negotiation.

Although life at sea in deep-water sailing ships can never have been very comfortable, working conditions on the coastal traders were as good as one could expect to find at sea in sailing vessels of this period. The captains were local men, the crews were few in number, well-known to and frequently related to one another, a tradition that persisted into the 19th and 20th centuries. Crews often fared better for food aboard ship than they would have done ashore: voyages were brief and plenty of fresh food could be bought. Certainly the items listed in Dr Lewis Lloyd's studies of the disbursement books of the Unity of Barmouth and the Amity of Aberdyfi, suggest a much more varied diet than that enjoyed by farming families for many years to come. The Unity's records cover the years 1781-1799 and those of the Amity, 1803-1809. Of even greater interest are the accounts of the brig Susannah of Aberdyfi, which cover the years 1815-1843, the early part corresponding to a period of hardship among the agricultural population. The earlier disbursement books refer to herrings, salmon, beef, mutton and plenty of fresh vegetables: potatoes, cabbages, onions, turnips and peas. The Susannah's books include potatoes, cheese, oatmeal, bread, fish, beef, pork, mutton, as well as the occasional purchase of chickens and geese; certainly a diet higher in protein than that generally eaten ashore. In the 1820s an able seaman earned £2 a month with all food provided; an ordinary seaman about 30 to 35 shillings a month and a boy 15 shillings a month. The mate would get about £3 and the master £5.

A picture of unrelieved gloom has been painted of the countryside in the years following the Battle of Waterloo, when the inflated wartime prices fell sharply at a time when hundreds of soldiers were thrown out of employment. Peter Thomas, whose book Strangers in a Secret Land deals with one solution to the problem, emigration, blames much of the trouble on the greed of the farmers who had exhausted the land by excessive cropping to meet the demand caused by Napoleon's blockade, a situation which recurred again in World War II with submarines playing the role taken earlier by privateers. Many farms were given up along the River Teifi and David Davies, Moylon, mentioned earlier, recorded the misery he saw all around him in another letter to his son. On 18th March 1816, less than a year after the Battle of Waterloo, he wrote: "As to country news I have not one (sic) good news to give you, the Agricultural product is quite a Drug, every Article the Farmer can spare is of little value. Good wheat sells at Newcastle (Emlyn) market for 5/- the Winchester Bushel, what I have seen sold for 20/-. Fine barley at 2/-, oats at 1/-, best butter at 8d per lb. Welch (sic) cheese at 3d, pork 3d, beef 4d, mutton 5d and so everything is in proportion except when we go to the country shops everything is as dear as ever. The farmers cannot pay their rents, in consequence of the high prices of the commodities of late years. The landed Proprietors in general are very cruel to their tenants - they give them up to the attorneys and the attorneys send their Bailiffs with Distress warrants to distrain upon the poor tenants, and bring their goods etc to Newcastle and sell 'em off for almost nothing... the Bailiffs are daily in the country like carrion crows or kites taking away everything... Great numbers of the tenantry here have already given up their farms against next Michaelmas. You know the most part of them. What will become of the country at last I cannot tell but the state of things look very black now. It is impossible for any man to assist a friend in need, for there is no money to be had, upon any sort of securities, they have of late sent (a) great many debtors to Cardigan gaol."(18) Worse was to come for the weather was so appalling that summer that the harvest failed everywhere. On 7th June 1817, when stocks were exhausted, before the next harvest had come in, David Williams of Bronmeurig wrote: "The Overseers (of the poor) testify to their total inability to keep them alive and call to God to witness that it is so - if they distress as they constantly do (seize goods for non-payment of poor relief by the farmers) they can get no money for what they seize. The poor are attempting to prolong life by swallowing barley-meal and water, boiling nettles etc and scores in the agony of famine have declared to me this week that they have not made a meal for two days together."(19)

Other landlords were more reasonable but the situation still remained a difficult one for farmers. Owen Richards, my great-great-great-grandfather, was farming on the Trawscoed estate during the Napoleonic wars. The rent of his farm, Dol-fawr, had been £72/10/- a year in 1801; by 1807, thanks to wartime demands for increased productivity, he was paying £200 rent annually. At this time, as Wilmot Vaughan, Earl of Lisburne, was a lunatic, his affairs were managed by his half-brother John Vaughan, who was answerable to Chancery.

In 1814, John Vaughan obtained permission to have the estate surveyed and valued by Adam Murray of St Martin's Lane, London with a view to increasing the rents yet again when the 7 year leases were re-negotiated and as one can see from the survey among the Trawscoed papers at the National Library an additional £3,000 a year was obtained. However, only two years later, John Vaughan was declaring to the Lord Chancellor that the tenants could no longer pay the high rents: "he knows all the tenants well, they are good and respectable people and it is not their fault". Despite a sympathetic landlord, Owen Richards decided to surrender his farm in 1821, and it is significant that he chose eventually to settle in Llanllwchaearn parish on the 240 acre farm of Nant-y-pelau, which was owned by Mr Jenkin Beynon of Llaethlliw, near Aberaeron, another landowner who took a great interest in the development of New Quay, as will be seen in Chapter II. Owen had a large family of children, mainly daughters, who married local farmers, among them John Davies of Gwaun-yr-efail, who became a timber merchant in Aberystwyth, while his mother ran the family farm. Thereafter the family's fortunes became bound up with that of the port of New Quay and his descendants settled there.

In the very same year that David Williams was writing about the dreadful conditions he witnessed, New Quay was launching its most ambitious vessel to date. In her size and rig, the 92 ton brig, Friendship, square-rigged on both masts, was in a very real sense a pioneer and became something of a mascot for the port. It is therefore most appropriate that she appears on the coat of arms subsequently devised for New Quay, along with three herrings, another mainstay of the port's prosperity at this time. The Friendship was built for the North American timber trade, which had grown considerably as a result of Napoleon's economic blockade of the Baltic, which meant that their supplies of timber from that area fell drastically with serious results for the shipping industry.

British merchants were initially reluctant to invest in alternative sources in Canada without some security, so prohibitive duties were placed on Baltic timber, which meant that even after the war ended it was worth importing timber from Quebec and the eastern provinces of Canada. On outward voyages the Friendship also sometimes carried emigrants from up-country, so in a sense profiting from the disaster.

Whatever the conditions prevailing inland, the Llanllwchaearn and Llandysuliogogo farmers were able to weather the storm, and those who had been farming before and during the war were still prospering, even after the succession of bad harvests in the 1820s. Possibly their investments in shipping helped them over this difficult time and certainly for them and for many others, emigration was far from being the only solution. From rural Llanllwchaearn, Llandysuliogogo and

Llannarth parishes and further afield, young men left their farms and smallholdings and came to New Quay to serve in its ships. Men in other trades quickly followed them.

An examination of the Censuses taken from 1801 onwards of the population of each parish indicates the steady growth of Llanllwchaearn's population. In 1801 the total was 678; Llannarth, its much bigger neighbour, with 15044 acres as opposed to Llanllwchaearn's 3249, had a population of 1719. Over the next decades both parishes increased their population, though Llannarth's having peaked in 1831 declined thereafter. However by 1851 Llanllwchaearn's had more than doubled with 1738 inhabitants, while Llannarth's population stood at 2337. The Census enumerators ascribed the increase in Llanllwchaearn in 1821, when the population reached 966, to the revival of the herring fishing, but it must also have owed something to the steadily growing number of ships possessed by the port of New Quay. By 1841, when the population had reached 1475 they admitted it was due to the erection of buildings at the Port of New Quay, a little closer to the point though rather oddly expressed. Of course the Census at that time simply indicated that a person was born in the County, in 1851 one could see that inward migration from 27 Cardiganshire parishes had swelled the population.

Cefn Gwyddil is a farm of 240 acres, a few miles from New Quay. At this time it was farmed by David Rees. He found that it paid to send his son John to sea, and he became master of the New Quay sloop Good Hope, launched in 1828. In Llandysuliogogo, similarly, Thomas

Owen, yeoman of Penparc, Cwmtudu, a 140 acre farm, found it worth his while to let his only son, Owen, go to sea. Their neighbours at Pendderw and Ciliau could easily provide him with a berth in one of the vessels in which they had invested. Owen remained at sea for twenty years until his father died in 1835 and he "swallowed the anchor" and took over the farm. Men with farming backgrounds seemed to have had no difficulties in mingling with both worlds. The Bee, built in New Quay in 1827, was commanded by Captain Thomas Davies from the little inland village of Nanternis, and her shareholders included Daniel Griffiths, Ty-hen, Llwyndafydd and Thomas Williams, Cyffionos, then known as Cwmffinos, a farm near Nanternis. From generation to generation, this tradition of a family combining seafaring or maritime investment and farming persisted.

Chapter II

The Harbour Company and the building of the Pier

In the same year that Owen Owen retired from the sea, plans were afoot at last to build a pier at New Quay. Schemes for a pier had been discussed in the 1790s when the pioneer agriculturist, the Rev Lewis Turnor, had urged the construction of a pier and the creation of an Irish packet station at New Quay. It was claimed that "ships of considerable burthen might come hither and with the assistance of the pier might ride safe in all weathers". Walter Davies, in his General View of the Economy of South Wales published in 1815, reinforced the argument: "By means of a pier at New Quay many useful lives might be saved...". It was stressed that New Quay offered a safer haven than anywhere else on this coast, since Barmouth, Aberdovey, Aberystwyth and Cardigan were all "barred", so only accessible at certain states of the tide. Walter Davies envisaged an expenditure of £30,000 "to secure two hundred ships at Carreg Ina". He clearly imagined a much bigger harbour than was eventually created, accessible at all states of the tide, but this was impossible given the impoverished state of Cardiganshire. In fairness to Walter Davies, he envisaged money coming in from outside investors such as Lloyds, since the pier would benefit all shipping in the heavily used sea-lanes on the approach to Liverpool. Had investment been on this scale, no doubt New Quay's history as an active port would have been of much longer duration.

If £30,000 seemed prohibitive, the scheme suggested by the famous engineer, John Rennie, who built the harbour at Birkenhead, was in the realms of cloud-cuckoo-land. In 1820, the Rev Alban Thomas Jones Gwynne of Aberaeron, who had already in 1807 obtained a Harbour Act for Aberaeron (1), turned his benevolent attention to New Quay and it was he who engaged John Rennie to draw up plans for the proposed pier. The figures Rennie quoted were £72,000 for a more elaborate scheme than that proposed by Walter Davies and £50,000 for a "harbour of asylum only". Inevitably the enterprise lapsed. In 1833 John R Haslam, Surveyor to the Royal Board of Ordnance, was invited to draw up plans and he came up with a much more affordable figure of under £3,000 although in retrospect this does not seem very realistic. However the Harbour Company was gradually taking shape in the minds of several local gentlemen and we can trace its growth and activities in the handsome red leather-bound book entitled in gold: New Quay Harbour Company Proceedings, preserved at the National Library of Wales (2).

On Tuesday, 30th June 1835, an important meeting was held at the Black Lion Inn, Lampeter, called for the express purpose of founding the New Quay Harbour Company. Captain James Richard Lewes Lloyd of Dol-haidd,

Carmarthenshire was appointed Chairman, Mr William Hall of Cardigan was appointed Clerk of the Company gratuitously for one year and the other directors were John Beynon Esq of Adpar Hall; David Arthur Saunders Davies Esq of Pentref, Pembrokeshire; the Rev David Evans of Llannarth, clerk; Alban Thomas Jones Gwynne Esq of Mynachdy; John Hughes of Alltlwyd Esq.; George Bowen Jordan Jordan Esq of Pigeonsford, Llangrannog; John William Lewis Esq of Llanaeron; Thomas Lloyd Esq of Coedmor, who was married to Charlotte Longcroft of Llanina; her brother Charles Richard Longcroft Esq; John Lloyd Esq. of Alltyrodyn; Francis David Saunders Esq of Ty Mawr, Cilcennin and Mr Evan Timothy of New Quay. It will be observed that, apart from William Hall, Evan Timothy was the only one who was not a landed proprietor. Many of the others were descendants of ancient Welsh families, the Lloyds of Coedmor, for instance, could trace their ancestry back over eight hundred years, though David Saunders Davies was the son of a doctor and grandson of a wealthy ironmonger. Most of them were connected by marriage. Thomas Lloyd could afford to subscribe £1,000 in shares and Charles Longcroft £200 though the rest subscribed £100 each including Evan Timothy. The directors' renumeration was not to be more than £30 per annum.

Who was Evan Timothy and how had he managed to 'crash' this exclusive society? So far, comparatively little is known of his early life: his descendants, however, are certain that he came from Ireland where he had been in the customs service and was probably posted to New Quay during the Napoleonic Wars, since his son David was born here in 1809. Like a number of the coastguards,

Evan Timothy identified himself very closely with his new home and eventually left the service and set up business in New Quay. He was closely associated, as we have seen, with Tabernacle Chapel. His first wife died and he married Elizabeth Walters in about 1818, whose father was the tenant of Goytre Farm, Llannarth and Evan himself appears to have farmed at Cefn-cwrt, Llangrannog in the 1820s as his name appears on the jury of the Court Leet for the Manor of Caerwedros.(3) They had a large family of sons and daughters, the former going into business in New Quay and the latter marrying local men so that in time the 'Timothiaid' figure significantly in New Quay's history. Today nearly all the old families have some Timothy connections. Between them the Timothys ran three shops in New Quay and Evan also invested in a number of ships. Evan and Elizabeth ran a large shop at the top of Pengeulan while Thomas Timothy had a draper's shop at 10 Pen-y-wig Row and David Timothy had another shop at 12 Pengeulan. When Evan died, his will, proved in 1850, was administered through the Prerogative Court of Canterbury because of his extensive business interests covering several counties and he left goods and chattels valued at £2,000. In 1835 he was 50 years old. The other members of the Harbour Company may have lent their names and long squirearchical tradition to the venture but it was Evan Timothy, assiduously attending meetings, who kept the undertaking on its feet.

The logical place to erect the pier was obviously on Pen-y-wig reef which ran out to sea below Pen-y-wig Farm. It was then occupied by William Evans, grandson of the John Evans who purchased the estate originally. William

Elizabeth Timothy in Welsh costume, still worn in New Quay on special occasions. The broad-brimmed tall hat was characteristic of New Quay costume and many have survived here. They were made of rabbit fur, carefully treated, at Llangynfelyn in North Cardiganshire and there was also a hatter named Thomas Harry living in Llanydsuliogogo in 1826 who was a shareholder in the brig Friendship. Photo courtesy of the late Mrs Mair Thomas.

Evans, Penwig, and Evan Evans, Neuadd, were the men with whom the Harbour Company had to negotiate the purchase of the land on which to build the pier and the railway to carry stone from the quarry to be opened on Evan Evans' land, during the course of which the present Rock Street was created. Solomon Williams was appointed to open the quarry. He too was a former coastguard and a keen supporter of the enterprise. He was a North Wales man, born in 1789 at Abersoch, son of Griffith and Elizabeth Williams who kept a tavern. He served for a time on a revenue cutter as a young man and was posted to New Quay in 1810. According to W Davies, who wrote his obituary in Y Diwygiwr (4), he had been rather a godless youth given to bad language but was so enormously impressed by the sermon preached by a visiting minister, William Davies of Pontrhydfendigaid, on the text Matthew XVI verse 26: "What shall it avail a man if he has the whole world, to lose his soul?" that he was "born again" in the enthusiastic tradition of the early Methodists. In 1818 he married a fellow Methodist from Cardigan, but the following year he was posted away from New Quay to Ireland and he regretted his departure so much that he left the service and returned to New Quay, where he opened a shop in Ty Capel. In 1824, he became a deacon of Tabernacle. He had six children and his daughter Eleanor later kept the first post office in New Quay at the family home. Solomon Williams was a close friend of Captain Thomas Phillips, the young master of the Adelphoi of New Quay. Like many sea-captains he was a deeply religious man and would never leave port on a Sunday, however fair the wind. When away from home he corresponded with Solomon Williams on religious subjects, particularly the preaching of the minister, the Rev

H Rees of Ffos-y-ffin or the Rev J Jones, Tal-sarn, whom he had heard at a Gymanfa in Cardigan. His letters quoted in his obituary by Benjamin Evans of Llety John in Y Diwygiwr, show him to have been a deeply thoughtful man: unfortunately he was drowned on Monday 21st November 1836, on a voyage from Liverpool to Ireland, near Bardsey, when a huge wave swept over the vessel in a gale and he was lost overboard. He was twenty-six years old.

The design of the pier was based on a scheme submitted eventually by Daniel Beynon, a young engineer, who was commissioned to draw up a plan in 1834 and Mr Rees Williams Jones of Loughor, Glamorgan, was appointed Engineer of the Company at a salary of £500 for two years from 29th September 1835, though out of this sum he had to pay a Clerk of the Works: this was a Mr William Hopkin, who received a salary of £12/10/- a month. The Directors hoped to raise the sum of £7,000 it was estimated the pier would cost from the sale of £10 shares in three calls.

One of the first acts of the Company was to purchase from William Evans "the piece of land extending from Pen-y-wig Point along the shore to a line drawn from the East corner of Mr David Timothy's house to the West corner of the large Storehouse near the old Pier (Penpolion) and bounded on one side by the road from the Revenue Watch-house and on the other side by the sea, including the limekilns and small storehouse, near the old Pier." A liberal, in their view, initial offer of £105 being rejected, William Evans eventually received £199. David Timothy's house was about half-way up

Pengeulan, later Glanmor Terrace. William Evans further received £1 annual rent at Michaelmas for the use of the land for the railroad to the quarry.

In February 1836, the Directors met at the Black Lion in New Quay and inspected the work for the railway and for opening the quarries at Pencastell Hill (known now as Pengraig). The iron rails for the railway had cost £241/16/9 and by then it was almost complete, being finished on 8th March 1836. (A portion of the rails is preserved today alongside the Tourist Office). The Directors met monthly during the building of the pier but occasionally there was no quorum so business could not be transacted. On April 11th 1836, Solomon Williams also attended the meeting, which was dominated by discussion of a project mooted by George Jordan of Pigeonsford. New Quay Harbour Company's jurisdiction, by the Act of Parliament for the construction of the pier (William IV 5), extended from Pan Head in the south (Ynys Lochdyn) to Black Rock to the north, where it came up against the jurisdiction of the Aberaeron Harbour Company. George Jordan was anxious that the Company should also build a small pier at Pan Head, which he felt would provide a more convenient landing place for goods than the current risky method of coming ashore with the tide on the open sandy beach at Llangrannog. It was estimated that it would cost £340. However, none of the other Directors was willing to incur additional expense and it was eventually suggested rather artfully that Mr Jordan build the pier at his own expense and he would be reimbursed from the harbour dues at New Quay, in instalments. Nothing further was heard of the project.

On 12th May 1836 gloom was cast over the works when Solomon Williams was killed. He was wheeling a barrow-load of stones over some staging at Ogof Ffeiriad (Parson's Cave) near the end of the present Rock Street, to be lowered in baskets into the waiting barges, when the staging collapsed and he fell thirty-five feet on to the rocks. He was knocked unconscious but recovered his senses in a few moments though severely injured. He was borne home by a sorrowing, silent crowd and died three hours later. His funeral the following Saturday was attended by a vast crowd for he had been a most popular man. This appears to have been the only fatal injury caused during the construction of the pier, although £3 was paid for the surgeon's bill in attending Josiah Rees "when injured at the Works". Nevertheless work continued. More flat-bottomed barges were being built at New Quay ready to transport the stone for the pier out into deeper water and R W Jones was authorised to purchase these for forty guineas. By 12th July the pier or "rough breakwater" as it was then called, was seventy-nine yards long.

By November, R W Jones had received sums amounting to £2,218/11/6 of which the greater part had been expended in wages; nearly £1400 to date. Unfortunately, the number of men employed is not given but smiths received 4/- a day, masons 2/6, carpenters 2/- and labourers 1/8. Women labourers were also employed, clearing the beach. In the winter months, when travelling was exceedingly uncomfortable, the monthly meetings were cancelled, recommencing 9th March 1837 in Cardigan and a fourth call for £2/10/- was made to subscribers. Oliver Lloyd of Cardigan was now the

The Quarry, opened at New Quay for stones to build the pier and from which also came the stone to build the many new houses erected thereafter. Courtesy of the National Library of Wales.

Chairman of the Company and its solicitor, and it was "resolved that in consequence of it appearing to the directors that the breakwater should be carried out further than the original capital of the company will enable them to do that the Chairman be requested to apply to the Exchequer Loan Office for an advance by way of loan of Three Thousand Pounds, which the company were empowered by their Act to borrow, in order to perfect and complete the work."

Indeed it seemed likely that the work would come to a halt for lack of funds. However they were able to keep going on their personal sureties and it was decided that Dues and Tolls should be collected from 1st October 1837. It was then that the list of dues was affixed to the harbour wall, drawn up by a Committee consisting of Patrick Brown of Cardigan, John Evans of Morfa Gwyn and Evan Timothy. The cost of painting the List of Tolls and Dues was £19. Mr James Davies of "Dole", New Quay, was appointed to collect the dues and tolls; a temporary appointment until the works were completed. He was to receive a salary of £45 a year and at his own expense to provide a boat and an assistant for the duties of his office whenever required.

The Directors had to mortgage the works to raise £1500 as the Exchequer Loan proved too expensive, and they advanced further sums from their own pockets. Thomas Lloyd gave £200, Charles Longcroft £150, Evan Timothy (now promoted to Esq in the accounts) a further £100 and Dr David Rowland of Chatham, brother-in-law of Mr Evan Evans, Penrhiwgaled, £150; an additional £1,000 was raised by this means and

The Tables of Tolls at New Quay. This is a later version than that originally erected and has since been protected by a glass case. Thomas Davies, the then Harbour Master, was formerly the Master of the Mary Hughes, a schooner built in New Quay in 1842, and lost off Cape Finistere in 1860, the crew being saved. Author's collection.

Thomas Lloyd lent a further £300 over three years. Up to May 1838, the Pier had brought in £129/18/7and a halfpenny in tolls and as the Works were swallowing money, it was decided to add an additional toll on limestone, one of the most frequently landed cargoes at New Quay, being used as a fertiliser on the land after being burnt in the limekilns. However the increase in the toll gave rise to complaints from the ship managers of which the brunt fell on James Davies and on his representation the dues were reduced on "all British vessels" to 2d a ton. On him now seems to have devolved the task of overseeing the last stages of the work and he reported on New Year's Day 1840 at a special General Meeting at the Black Lion in New Quay that he was "making the slip for timber" which must surely refer to the lowest level of the pier, the slip by the storehouse, the latter being erected soon after at a cost of £176/18/10 and for many years was let to John Rees and his son as a sail-loft. A light was subsequently erected on the Pierhead and in 1848 Jenkin Evans was being paid fifty shillings annually for "attending and lighting the Pierhead lamp".

In 1839 the Harbour dues had brought in £181//10. This was promising but when one considers that there were borrowings of almost £3,000 secured on this income, in addition to the fact that the shareholders would naturally expect some return on their investment, it was not a great deal. Perhaps that is why the Company decided to auction the tolls to the highest bidder, which would at least assure them of a lump sum to pay off the debts and it would be an incentive to collect the tolls more assiduously. This, of course, was the procedure followed by the Welsh Toll-gates and led, through the greed of the toll-collectors, to the Rebecca Riots. The first attack at a toll-gate at Efail-wen, Pembrokeshire, had in fact occurred on 13th May 1839. Fortunately, in New Quay, people seem to have been content merely to grumble occasionally. On 24th March 1840, the tolls were let by auction to Mr Jenkin Beynon, Llacthlliw, Henfenyw; and Mr Evan Evans, Towyn Farm, for £276, to be paid quarterly. As the auction took place at the Black Lion, the accounts record 10/- paid to Mr John Patrick for a bowl of punch. Thereafter the more frequent meetings were abandoned and the Directors met annually for the auction of the tolls.

The Harbour was built none too soon for already in the last two decades 72 ships had been launched at New Quay, double the number of the previous two decades. The next chapter considers this enormous increase in shipbuilding activity since 1800.

Chapter III

Shipwrights and Shareholders

When one considers that more than 200 vessels were built in New Quay between 1778 and 1890, it may seem surprising that so little trace of these shipyards remains. However, as Basil Greenhill points out in Westcountrymen in Prince Edward's Isle: "Shipyards were less shipyards in the modern sense than sites where a master builder could put a vessel together and rig her, working slowly with the aid of a few men less skilled than himself" (1)

In The Merchant Schooners, he amplifies this statement: "Right until the last days of their construction in the present century, the greater number of merchant schooners... were built... under the most primitive conditions...In such a yard there would be at the most two and perhaps only one sawpit with a single pair of sawyers... (and) they would ...put up a shack or two at some generally convenient point on the coast..."(2) Once the yard was abandoned, sand would fill up the sawpits and the huts would be dismantled.

Ships were not required to be registered until 1786, so before that date we have few details of who built the ships and where they were launched. It seems probable that only a handful of ships were built here before 1800. But in the first two decades of the new century thirty-four vessels were built here, all save three being sloops ranging from 8 to 73 tons, although more usually around 20-30 tons.(3) The sloop or smack, a single-masted vessel, fore-and-aft rigged with a gaff topsail from the topmast and a jib, perhaps a flying jib from a running bowsprit, was the most common rig for the small merchant sailing ship in Britain in the 1700s and the first half of the 1800s. However, the two-masted fore-and-aft schooner rig was known in New Quay by 1810 and eventually became a very popular rig for coasting vessels with 97 being launched here along with over 100 sloops. Between 1820 and 1840, 72 vessels were launched in New Quay, twice as many it will be observed, as in the previous two decades. In the Shipping Register at Aberystwyth a distinction was made between yards at Traethgwyn, Cei Bach and New Quay, which were all operating at the same period. The earliest identified shipbuilder at Traeth-gwyn was the farmer-sailor cum entrepreneur, who was one of the men responsible for drawing up the Table of Tolls for the Harbour. John Evans, (1789-1871) was the son of a farmer, Francis Evans, who farmed at Penllwybr on the Llannarth-Llanina border and at Penrhiwpistyll, Llanllwchaearn, later on and died there in 1817. John was one of six brothers, Evan (1784-1847), who farmed Penllwybr, Griffith who farmed Penrhiwpistyll till his death in 1831; Job (1791-1844) who farmed at Llaingrog; Morgan, Master Mariner, White Hart, Pengeulan, (1804-1863); Francis Evans, Penrhiwpistyll (1806-1863). In 1816, when he was only 26, John launched the biggest sloop yet recorded in New Quay, the 73 ton Eleanor; she was his own vessel and he commanded her for several years, trading with Ireland and building up his capital - he had an occasional brush with the Customs and Excise, but prospered. He owned a limekiln on Traethgwyn beach and a malthouse at Glyngolau and he also had shares in the sloop Delegate, 17 tons, built the same year as the Eleanor, and in the Venus, built at neighbouring Cei Bach in 1820. The little 9 ton sloop Flying Fish was built by him in 1820 and may have been a fishing boat.

In 1829 John commissioned Thomas Davies, who later rented a shipyard from him by the public-house the Shipwright's Arms, to build him, a 54 ton sloop, the Catherine, at a cost of £886/12/- .(4) By 1831 he and his younger brother Francis were in a position to buy Penrhiwpistyll and Glyngolau, which included the waterfront at Traethgwyn, for £3,700 and while Francis farmed at Penrhiwpistyll, John built himself the house known as Morfa Gwyn and farmed along with pursuing his shipping interests. On 6th March 1833 the house was ready for roofing and the Venus brought in 3,600 Cilgerran slates from Cardigan. In February 1834, the Catherine was paying a profit of £11a share and the Eleanor brought in higher returns: in the same year she paid £63/19/11 three farthings on 3/16ths.

Shares in ships were divided into sixty-four parts or sixteen ounces, each ounce equivalent to four shares, so three sixteenths represented three shares. It was a higher return than one could expect from shore-based investments and it emboldened John to commission yet another vessel, the Nell, from Thomas and John Davies, Traethgwyn. This was a 57 ton sloop. Part of the contract has survived and reads: "John Evans, please to pay to my father Thomas Davies of the sign of the Shipwrights Arms at Newquay the sum by Instalments as follows towards the building of a New Vessel by me John Davies, Bilder at Traethgwin for you and the other share owners, Thirty-two pounds when the foot and stem and flourings laid in, forty pounds when frames and keelson laid in, forty-eight pounds when planked to the bends and Bends laid in, Fifty-six pounds when the hull is completed ready for launch. The remainder part of payment at the seignment of the Bill of Sale... 23 November 1833".

John had to borrow from his brother Job to pay for the Nell which was not launched until 1835. But if John had many calls on his purse he had a steady income coming in, not only from his ships, but also rents from the cottages he owned at Traethgwyn and Brongwyn Street, inhabited mostly by the men who worked in the shipyards of Traeth-gwyn. The yard of Thomas Davies brought in £2 a year and the rent for the Shipwright's Arms was a further £2 and was sometimes paid in kind, for example 28 barrels of "lamskin culm" at £1/16/8. The cottages paid about £1/8/- a year. At this time and for many years to come, the main and only road from New Quay to Aberaeron led down Brongwyn Street, past Morfa Gwyn to Llanina, whence it forked, one branch going to Pencroescastell on the Cardigan Road, and another via Gilfachreda to Llannarth. Erosion has removed much of Morfa Gwyn's land and of the smallholding of Maesgwyn which once stood on the opposite side of the road and was still lived in until the early 1940s, nothing now remains and the old road has disintegrated beyond Brongwyn Street.

Thomas Davies, born in Penbryn in 1783, was building vessels at Traethgwyn probably from at least 1810 as his son John was born in New Quay that year. He launched the Hope there in 1821 and the yard he established functioned until at least the 1860s under the guidance of his son John, who built the Active in 1848 with Daniel Thomas. Thomas Davies appears to have retired by that date, he was 68 in 1851, although he still describes himself as a ship's carpenter in the Census. John Davies's most ambitious ventures were the 130 ton brigantine Hawendale, launched in 1858, which went deepwater but was also employed in the coasting trade and his last vessel, another brigantine, the Keldhead, 132 tons, launched in 1862, which traded to the West Indies. The brigantine was a two-masted vessel square-rigged on the foremast and fore-and aft rigged on the main, usually the smallest type of square-rigged vessel and very graceful ships. He died that year.

Two other shipbuilders at Traethgwyn were also named Thomas Davies though one called himself Thomas Jenkin Davies to avoid confusion. Thomas Davies the second lived at the Red Lion, near Traethgwyn and was born in Llangrannog in 1791. He came to New Quay about 1830 as his daughter Eleanor was born there in 1831, but he does not appear to have begun building on his own until 1849 when he launched the schooner Ann & Mary, followed by the Affines in 1851, when he was employing ten men. He appears not to have launched another vessel until 1860, the 82 ton schooner, Rosina.

In 1864 Thomas Davies launched the schooner U'larsing, named for one of the first Indian converts made by Welsh missionaries (qv); and in 1866 possibly the brigantine Dreadnought which served for years in the Newfoundland trade. In 1902 she was lost off the coast of Peru with all hands, the last deepwater sailing vessel owned in New Quay. However one cannot be sure that her builder was this Thomas Davies, Red Lion, who would have been 76 years old by the time the Dreadnought was launched.

Thomas Jenkin Davies built five vessels between 1848 and 1859: three schooners, the brigantine Melodia and the three-masted barque Lettice Catherine, 293 tons, launched in 1859 for the South American trade and lost nine years later at Bahia Blanca. Barques were square-rigged on the fore and main masts and fore-and-aft rigged on the mizzen.

James Davies was a shipwright employed at Traethgwyn from 1840 onwards; he built two vessels, another Friendship in 1857 and the Julianna in 1864, both 79 ton schooners. Thereafter he was chiefly engaged in superintending repair work at the Patent Slip at New Quay (qv). The last vessel described as being built at Traethgwyn was a 97 ton schooner, the Clarita, built in 1870 by Thomas and David Davies: she survived until 1930, the last New Quay-built vessel still afloat.

Henry Watkins is the earliest identified shipbuilder at Cei Bach He had children baptised at Llanina in the 1780s. The earliest known vessel to be built there was the Rachel & Sally in 1803, a sloop of 30 tons, probably built for the family of Llwynon farm. James Davies built the sloop Eliza, 45 tons, in 1825. The really busy years at Cei Bach came later. Between 1836 and 1851, a shipbuilder named Thomas Thomas worked there, launching the schooners Elizabeth, Pearl, Phillip, Esther & Mary, Sisters, Perseverance, Eleanor and Martin. The last three were on the stocks at virtually the same time in 1848.

In 1849 he launched his only brigantine, the Revival, 136 tons. His last vessel was the schooner Integrity launched in 1851. He lived on until 1866 but his name is not associated with any new vessel. Thomas James Thomas had begun to work at Cei Bach in 1850 with the 54 ton schooner Loyalty. He was then 39, and in 1851 was employing thirteen journeymen, that is men who had completed their apprenticeship. Among them was Lewis Jones, Pier, Cei Bach which may refer to the stone and metal barrier which still remains between Cei Bach and the Llethi river. Then there was Jacob Evans, Cwm Penrhiwgaled, whose father was a cobbler; the David Williamses, father and son of Ffynnonfeddyg: David Williams, senior, was 66 in 1851 and may well have worked on ships at Cei Bach all his working life. Another was David Evans, Cwm Noyadd, born in Llannarth; and David and Jenkin Evans from Gilfachreda, whose father was a pauper cobbler. Thomas Thomas also came from an impoverished background as his father David was a pauper agricultural labourer who had moved here from Llandysuliogogo. They lived at Llain Ty Simne, a group of now ruined cottages below Five Oaks Cottage, between Gilfachreda and Cei Bach. Another journeyman was Evan Williams, Llaingarreglwyd, whose father was also an

The schooner Martin, photographed at Eu, Normandy. She had a bird for a figurehead. Courtesy of Mr Aneurin Moller.

agricultural labourer from Llannarth. The antecedents of these men clearly demonstrate the possibility of advancement in status and prosperity provided by the shipbuilding boom. Finally there was Evan Daniel Evans, 28, who lodged with his aunt, a labourer's widow, in Salamanca, a cottage near Cnwc-y-lili, probably named to commemorate the Duke of Wellington's great victory in Spain in 1812. Evan Daniel, as he was known, would become the last active shipbuilder in the district, dying in 1890. He also may have been among the last examples of the use of the patronymic, adopting his father's Christian name as his surname.

Thomas James Thomas built thirteen ships between 1850 and 1866 when he died at the comparatively young age of 56. He was the most ambitious of the district's builders, launching the first barque, Prince Llewelyn, 286 tons, in 1858, built for the South American trade to the nitrate ports, in which she sailed for twenty-five years, rounding Cape Horn many times before her shipwreck in 1883 off St Thomas in the West Indies. He also built another barque, the Syren, 291 tons, the following year, whose story will be related later on when discussing the deepwater trade.

In 1855 Evan Daniel began to build on his own account at Cei Bach. Between then and 1882 he launched fifteen vessels, both coasting trade schooners and deepwater brigs, including New Quay's last schooner, the Owny Belle, for John Owen, Ciliau & Co., faithful investors for three-quarters of a century, along with farming in the Cwm Tudu valley; and the Maggie Phillips, 165 ton brigantine launched in 1878. She traded to South

America with coal from Cardiff and brought back sugar. Her master was Thomas Evans of New Quay.

John Evans built the Emma Alice, an 83 ton schooner, for himself at Cei Bach in 1867. It was not unusual for a man to build just one ship, since he could hire the skilled labour he needed to carry out the work and no-one knew better than her Master how a ship should perform. John kept 23 shares in her, selling the remainder and was her master and managing owner until he retired and sold her to Dublin in 1890. The managing owner was responsible for arranging cargoes. Many masters had shares in more than one vessel, like Jenkin Phillips. He was born in New Quay in 1750 and had seven children. When he died in 1821, he left "one quarter of the sloop Hopewell" to his son Thomas Phillips and "ten ounces of the sloop called Spread Eagle" to his son John; and his "three ounces in the sloop Heart of Oak" to his surviving daughters, one each to Margaret Thomas, Mary Jenkins and Elinor Davies. Jenkin's grandson, another Jenkin Phillips, (1801-1884), became master of the Ifor in 1854 and lived at 9 High Terrace which he named Ifor House. Besides shares in the Ifor, he had extensive holdings in the U'larsing, the Maggie Phillips and the Utopia. His cousin, John Phillips, master of the schooner Marys, left his wife twenty-eight shares when he died in 1869; and other relatives, the Evan Phillipses, who lived at 8, Marine Terrace, were heavy investors, both in ships and later in the Patent Slip. The 'Phillipiaid', like the 'Timothiaid' and the 'Gofion', were one of New Quay's old-established 'tribes'.

A contemporary, Jenkin Phillips, no relation, lived at the Glyn and was a Master Mariner until he retired to become a merchant and draper, owning shares in at least 12 vessels and managing many of them. (6) Very few people owned ships outright, unless they were fairly small and perhaps old vessels, which they crewed themselves with a mate, like Thomas Owen from Llangrannog parish, who bought the 29 ton smack Union Packet of New Quay in the 1860s, when she was forty years old and carried cargoes of slates and coal around Cardigan Bay.

The earliest known builder in connection with a particular vessel in New Quay, was James Thomas, who built the Aunt in 1831. This rather unusual name may have been occasioned by his having been brought up by an aunt as his mother died in his infancy. He was born in New Quay, in 1776, the son of the then curate of New Quay, the Rev Thomas Parry; his half-brother George Parry, taught a Sunday School at Penrhiwgaled Chapel from 1810 till his death in 1817. He was a shopkeeper, but James always seems to have been at sea. Unfortunately, the Aunt was lost in 1838. James's son John was also a mariner and at this time was living in Liverpool and voyaging from there, lodging in the rather notorious Dennison Street, where knife fights were common among seamen at the many lodging-houses. John married a Liverpool Scot and eventually came home to New Quay to command the 44 ton sloop Velocity, before becoming one of New Quay's pilots, employed to guide in vessels unfamiliar with the harbour. His cottage gave its name to Pilot Place, a little lane leading down from George Street to the Black Lion: the cottages there, now replaced by garages, commanded an excellent view of the sea.

Another one-off builder was David Simon, who built the smack Myra, 31 tons, in 1832. Most of her shareholders were farmers from Llansantffraid. But the doyen of New Quay shipbuilders was David Davies, who came from Penbryn as a young man to work in New Quay, perhaps with his brother, Thomas Davies, who had a yard at Traethgwyn. By 1833, David was working on his own account and living at Ty'r Angel, a former public-house at the junction of a network of little lanes connecting Pengeulan, High Terrace and Church Street, behind Penwig farmhouse. He built at least fifteen vessels, mostly schooners, but also the little sloop, Eliza & Mary, in 1840. He died in 1861 aged 86. Some of his vessels were built in conjunction with his son Thomas, including the schooners John & Mary, Ceretica and Louisa Ann. The Ceretica became a total loss only two years after her launch when she struck Copeland Island in thick fog, on a voyage from Limerick to Liverpool in 1851.

Other New Quay shipbuilders were John Davies, Evan Evans, John Rees and David Evans. (7) Owen Owen, who lived at 5, North Terrace, New Quay, built his vessels on Traethgwyn beach since at that time there was no space for another yard at New Quay. Like Thomas and David Davies, he had been born in Penbryn, in 1805, and came to New Quay as a young man, when skilled shipwrights were in demand. He was still a journeyman in 1841, but in 1850 he launched the first of his four vessels, the 125 ton schooner Ellen Catherine. In the Census of 1851 he listed himself as the employer of four men and it is probable that he and those four built the Ellen Catherine, with the aid of casual labour as required. Only 19 men actually described themselves as shipwrights and ships' carpenters in New Quay in 1851. Although in earlier accounts of the history of New Quay,(8) the figure of 300 has been mentioned in connection with those employed in shipbuilding, a survey of the Censuses for this and neighbouring districts like Llanina and Cytblwyf has failed to produce a total anywhere near that figure, even allowing for casual labour and one must conclude that it was produced under a misapprehension as to the number actually required to build the many vessels produced by New Quay in these years: up to four or five vessels annually and even ten occasionally, plus repairs to others, which must have offered continuous employment.

Shipbuilding was an expensive business, especially ensuring that sufficient stocks of seasoned timber were available. Timber lay seasoning in Cae Blociau (now a car park near the District Council offices and known as Paragon yard, and before that a hayfield, when it ceased to be used as a timber yard) for years, so the builders seldom had much liquid capital. However only one ship builder is known to have gone bankrupt: Thomas Davies of New Quay, in 1855. Nevertheless, the men who made the most profit from their ships were not the builders so much as the Master Mariners who, as we have seen, often held large numbers of shares in their vessels, and the tradesmen who could afford to invest on a large scale.

Timber for New Quay's ships came from overseas on board the Friendship and other New Quay vessels, but a good deal was home-grown and supplied by merchants from Cardiganshire, Carmarthenshire and Brecon, hauled into New Quay on huge wagons drawn by eight horses. Among the merchants who supplied timber was David Evans, Neuadd and Frondolau, who provided timber for the schooner Affines, for example, built in 1851, and a new Friendship, launched in 1857. John Jones of Garnfoel, Cardiganshire, supplied timber for the Jane, a 77 ton schooner built in 1844. William Williams, timber merchant of Brecon and John Jones, of Sennybridge, both supplied timber for re-building the smack Mary Jane, when she was lengthened in 1855. Daniel Thomas, "Disgyl Rock", near New Quay, supplied timber for the New Quay-owned Magdalen Esther, built in Aberaeron in 1857. Thomas Jones, timber merchant of Aberystwyth, supplied timber for the barque Syren, launched in 1859. The little Dandy schooner Thomas & Sons, was named for Thomas Thomas, Llandeilo Fawr, a timber merchant who owned 32 shares in her. Another Carmarthenshire timber merchant was Daniel Williams of Pen-y-bont, who supplied the wood for the Ann & Margaret, a 76 ton schooner launched in 1859. John Prothero of "The Walton", Brecon, was the supplier for at least seven New Quay vessels built in the 1860s: the Newfoundland trader William Landreth and the Gertrude, both brigs, built in 1863; the big 186 ton schooner U'Larsing, in 1864; in 1865 the brigs Ocean Dart and Isabel; another brig the Triton and the schooner Emma Alice, in 1867. All these merchants had shares in these ships. Evan Jones, timber merchant of Aberaeron, had shares in the Clarita in 1870.(9) Evan Timothy the younger, was the main supplier of timber in the 1870s: for the Maggie Phillips, the Melodia when she was lengthened and the Owny Belle.(10)

Chapter IV

Ancillary trades and the Growth of New Quay

The shipbuilding boom in New Quay peaked in the 1840s when 51 ships were built here and the effects of this boom spread out like ripples from a stone thrown into a pond. It attracted many men in ancillary trades, sail-making, rope-making, rigging and also craftsmen in other fields and shopkeepers to provide goods and services of all kinds. One of New Quay's major shareholders in ships and a man whose business grew along with the village, was John Jones, sail-maker. He was born in Cardigan in 1817, the son of a sail -maker there, Jonathon Jones. In the 1820s Jonathan was supplying sails for some of New Quay's vessels in which he himself invested: he had two shares in the Victory, for example, launched in Cei Bach; and when John had completed his apprenticeship, he advised his son to set up his business in New Quay. At the age of 34, he was living in one of the new houses recently built in what would become High Terrace, a house like many others which were changing the face of New Quay, stone houses built from the blue-grey stone of the quarry opened up to build the pier, with slate roofs, in wider streets than the narrow alleys around Penwig where the first cottages had been erected. John prospered sufficiently at his sail-making to build a larger house higher up the street. He married well too: Frances, one of the several daughters of Evan Timothy, the town's leading merchant and the guiding spirit behind the erection of the pier. In the 1851 Census John described himself as a Master Sail-maker, his sail-rooms being not far from his home, on the Front, in a tall building later known as the Pier Hotel, adjoining Penwig, in the street now named South John Street. John's sails were in demand not only in New Quay but also in Aberaeron, Aberdyfi and even as far away as Swansea. Fitting out a ship was an expensive business so perhaps it was not surprising that he was frequently paid for his sails in shares. He had a grand total of 123 shares in 40 ships at various times, representing an immense investment.

Another sail-making firm based in New Quay was that of John Edwards and his son James, who had their sail-rooms at Glyn Square. Like John Jones, John Edwards was born in Cardigan and his father Thomas had shares in New Quay ships from 1820 onwards. A third set of sail-rooms, in the storehouse on the pier, was run by John Rees and his son. For many years of course sails were sewn by hand, the men sitting on special benches in the large light room, each bench equipped with their tools, especially the palm, a leather hand protector designed to assist with pushing the heavy needle through the canvas. (An example can be seen at the Heritage Centre). Subsequently machines were introduced. There were said to be so many sail-making apprentices that they were able

John Jones, Sail-maker, (1817-1882). Courtesy of Mrs Mair Thomas.

to form a brass band. There was also a sail-maker at Hengell and years ago, before the new estate was built at Cwm Halen, the name Sailmaker could be still be traced on the gate leading to his cottage. (1)

Rope-making was carried on in New Quay first on the site of the future Water Street and down into Prospect Place. One of the earliest identified rope-makers was Evan Evans, who inherited Towyn farm though it was farmed by his brother David for a time. After Evan returned to farming in the 1840s, John Jones, who lived on Towyn land, became a rope-maker here. He too had been born in Cardigan where no doubt he learnt his trade and spent some time working in Merthyr Tydfil, South Wales, before moving to New Quay in the 1840s. By that time more houses were being erected and the Ropewalk was moved to the rear of Park Street. Another was subsequently set up behind Lewis Terrace on Neuadd land and the old rope house still stands there though it was damaged by fire some years ago. The photograph shows the interior before the fire.

"The yarns were first drawn through a copper of boiling Stockholm pitch then bound on bobbins and placed in a large frame where they revolved freely. They were then drawn through a board with a number of circularly placed small holes; then through a heated iron tube and fixed to the revolving pinion of the jack which had at one end a cogged iron wheel to which cogged pinions could be engaged. At the other end was a tapered grooved capstan cogged at the top and connected with the cogwheel. A strong rope, fastened at the other end of the walk, was placed around the capstan in a groove, a horse

Interior of the old rope house, New Quay. In the foreground is the stone-surrounded copper where the pitch was heated by a fire-place in the outside wall. A wooden roller appears in the wooden channel along which the ropes passed through holes in the window shutter, and there was a guillotine for cutting it. Richard Passmore stands on the step provided for the workers to superintend the pitch safely. Author's collection.

was hitched on and as it was led down the walk, the jack on wheels would be drawn along, causing the cogwheel to turn, thereby giving the right number of turns to the strand. When the three or four strands were made they were laced together and formed a rope".... "For spinning twines, a man with a large bundle of hempen fibres round his waist, walked backwards spinning a rope yarn."(2) Forty or fifty yards was need as a walk for spinning twines.

Blacksmiths too were much in demand to work on the ships and by 1851 there were six smithies in New Quay. At the Efail Fawr at this time worked David Davies, his brother Thomas, and nephew Owen. David was a deacon of Maen-y-groes Chapel and a rather scurrilous verse current for many years in New Quay ran:

Whip heibio'r cornel	Fast round the corner
Wrth yr Efail Fawr	By the Great Smithy
Mae Dafydd yn gweitho'n galed	David's working hard
A Twm yn feddw fawr.	And Tom is very drunk.

Owen's account book for the years 1866 to 1896 has been preserved and is full of references to work on the ships. It opens with a bill for work done by him on the Maria, David Davies's new schooner, which fills three closely written pages of the big ledger: totalling £161/15/8 and a half-penny. Page after page provides an invaluable record and many vessels' names recur over the years: the 'Passifick', Captain Jones' schooner, launched in 1859, often needed repairs: £31 was spent on her in 1866, £41 in 1867, £23 in 1872. The ledger is now at St

Fagan's Folk Museum in Cardiff, the owner at the time despairing of there ever being a museum in New Quay.

Owen Davies began his married life in the 1860s sharing a house with his in-laws who kept the Castle public-house in Church Street. By 1870 he had his own home in the newly-built Lewis Terrace, but then - like John Jones - he built himself something more handsome alongside, in 1881, the house named Bronwylfa. His daughter, surely uniquely among Victorian blacksmiths' daughters, learnt Greek, Latin and French at a boarding school in Swansea.

Another smithy was working above Penwig, the Efail Fach, which still stands just above White Street, and is now a holiday cottage. There was another over the Patent Slip, alongside the path leading down to Penpolion, rented from the Penwig Estate for 18/- a year; another stood across the road from the old Crown public-house at the upper end of Pengeulan and there was one at the quarry end of Rock Street and one at Traethgwyn. The last to survive was at Penrhiwllan on the road to Maen-y-groes. A son of this family acquired the soubriquet "Dai Chicago" when he emigrated in the twenties to that city and popular legend credited him with having driven cars for Al Capone during Prohibition. After standing empty for many years, the smithy was pulled down only a few years ago and has been replaced by a house.

At least three of the smiths were immigrants: Griffith Rees, the Pengeulan smith, was from Llansantffraid and married the daughter of the Crown in 1834; John Evans,

Morfa Gwyn, gave his servant Samuel 2/- to take to the bidding. It was customary for weddings to be announced by a 'bidder' carrying a decorated staff and guests brought money gifts to be reciprocated when they married or in return for gifts already given. In this way, newly-weds were given a good financial send-off. Weddings were frequently the excuse for some horse-play. A custom which persisted until well into the twentieth century is described by 'Ap Cei Newydd' in the Welsh Gazette in 1932: "While the wedding was at the church a 'Quinten' was erected across the road above Frondolau. The 'Quinten' was composed of thorns and other obstacles to prevent the party passing and I suppose that ransom had to be promised in the way of drink before the 'Quinten' was removed. It was always part of the fun of a wedding." More recently a rope was simply held across the road and the holders received a handful of silver to let the bridal car pass. Another custom was to hang out flags for a wedding so the village was often gaily bedecked.

John Peters, the smith at Quarry Row, was from Solva, Pembrokeshire, but he too married a local wife. Thomas Owen at Traethgwyn came from Penbryn but all his children were born in New Quay. This migration, which increased the population of New Quay immensely between 1830 and 1850, drew people from 27 Cardiganshire parishes alone, as well as from other Welsh counties and clearly demonstrates the attraction of New Quay's growing prosperity.(3) Eighty households were added to the town between 1841 and 1851. Like the sail-makers, the smiths had shares in the ships on which they worked. Owen Davies had shares in 18 ships. He also owned a fishing boat named John Bright, after the Radical politician. From the first, New Quay was radical in politics perhaps because it was inhabited largely by craftsmen and mariners and so relatively independent of the Tory landowners.

Other craftsmen essential in shipbuilding were the blockmakers, who made the variety of pulling blocks needed in sailing ships, some of immense size. There were two in the New Quay area: Owen Owen (who was born in Aberporth,) and John Jones, Hafod, Llanina. John Jones had two shares in the schooner Martin and four in the schooner Ruby, launched in 1856 at Cei Bach; he also had shares in the 118 ton schooner Gwalia, built at Aberaeron in 1852 and the 185 ton brig Crusader, also owned in Aberaeron, but built at Abeystwyth in 1865. In the 1870s he was listed in Lloyds' Register as the managing owner of these four vessels. (4)

In addition to the ships' carpenters, in 1851 there were 18 carpenters and joiners, engaged in fitting up the new houses with the masons, and constructing handsome furniture for cabins as well as homes. The carpenters also did a good deal of work on the farms and the following bill among John Evans, Morfa Gwyn's papers gives a good idea of the money they earned:

Making shaft one day 1/-
Making harrow one and a half days 1/9
Two days repairing cart 2/6
Making wheelbarrow one day 1/3
Sawing ash one day 1/3
Making new pair of wheels 18/-
Fixing axle-tree in smithy 2/6

The village was entirely self-sufficient: almost everything one needed for everyday life could be made on the spot: tools, clothes and shoes. Although there were several drapers in the town, in the mid-nineteenth century ready-made clothes were not that common and they mostly sold materials to be made up so tailors and dressmakers found plenty of employment. A number of people earned their living through processing wool for the hard-wearing Welsh flannel widely worn: running carding factories, spinning, weaving and stocking-knitting.

There were two 'factories' in the area: Nant-y-pelau Factory at Nanternis on the River Soden, near Nant-y-pelau mill, and the other near Gilfachreda on the road to Bwlch-cefn utilising the upper reaches of the Afon Gido for power. Both of these factories had water-driven scribbler carders which were introduced in the first decade of the 19th century. The factories were run by men from Llanfihangel-Genau'r Glyn: William Griffiths was at Nant-y-pelau and despite the name factory he was the sole employee and the same applied to Edward Oliver in Cytblwyf. Llanfihangel Genau'r Glyn had been a centre for woollen manufacture since the early 1800s when several mills were set up on the River Leri. By the 1840s the Leri Mills employed 35 weavers and probably William Griffith and Edward Oliver had decided to bring their skills to an area lacking in these resources. The Nant-y-pelau factory had ceased work by 1881 and Edward Oliver died in 1882.

The factories might have been supplied with wool by William Richards, Golan House, Gilfachreda, wool merchant, after 1870, though of course individual farmers would bring their own wool either to be carded for spinning at home or to be sold. The factories supplied wool for the weavers and the charge for carding was generally tuppence ha'penny a pound. Many people still carded their wool by hand: in 1796 Thomas Evan John of Llannarth was fully employed making hand carders for teasing impurities from wool and rendering it ready for spinners. He had an apprentice named Thomas Michael put to him by the parish at a charge of £1/7/6 a year.(5)

The carded wool if not spun at home, could have been spun by one of the six spinners in the parish. Spinning, if one had the skill, was a relatively cheap occupation to adopt, as the big wheel generally used cost as little as 5/- and "could be produced by any moderately skilful carpenter".(6) Spinners were often unmarried mothers, though it must be said that morals were not particularly lax in Llanllwchaearn parish and had probably improved since the early years of the century when, judging from the entries in the parish registers of Llanllwchaearn and Llanina, 'shotgun' or belated marriages were the norm. In a comparatively primitive, isolated society, less stigma was attached to pre-marital sex, though the spread of Nonconformity radically altered Welsh views as the century advanced. Another occupation practiced by poorer women was that of stocking-knitter and there were a couple of dozen of these in the area, mostly widows and spinsters.(7)

Hand looms were more expensive at £2 a loom and weaving seems to have been carried out by men only in this district. A weaver could reckon on weaving 25 yards a week and the woven cloth sold at about three or four pence a yard so earning not much above 8/- a week. Between 1841 and 1881 there were six weavers in the district: one of them, John Jones, had a weaving shop at Mason Street, up near Perth-y-gwenyn, for over 30 years. The weavers not only wove the cloth but also dyed the wool using, among other vegetable dyes, indigo for blues and greens, which was imported into New Quay; it appears on the Table of Tolls. "Nani Winllan" whose cottage, now vanished, stood on the lane from Fforchcwm, near Cross Inn, was one of the last people in the area to practice this ancient skill.(8) The local weavers generally 'fulled' the cloth themselves as well: this was the process of "closing together the threads of woven woollen fabric together with the assistance of soap or acid liquor"(9) and then 'tented' it, stretching it out to dry, though there was a Pandy (Fulling-mill) at Llannarth, pulled down some years ago, across the road from the old Tannery, which also carried on these functions. The Tannery of course prepared leather for local needs. Evan Jones also had a weaving shop in Mason Street in the first half of the 19th century and later at Pant-glas and David Jones worked at 1, Glyngolau. There were other weavers in Llanina and at Cross Inn.

The homespun material was made into garments by six tailors, who found employment in New Quay in the 1850s, from Llangeler, Troed-yr-aur, Solva and Llanddewi Aberarth, as well as two local men, one of whom was probably the son of Evan Jones, as he lived at Pant-glas, and another was William Williams, who lived in Brongwyn Street and gave it its nickname of Pentre

Sisiwrn. Isaac Davies lived at Maen-y-groes and worked for John Evans, Morfa Gwyn. In the latter's account books we find the following entries:

1843 Feb 25 Making and mending 3/7

1844 Isaac work one day Francis clothes and Nell 3/0 (these were John's children)

1845 May 28 Isaac making coat waistcoat trousers to myself 5/- making gown to Mary 1/- (his wife)

Several of the younger, unmarried women worked as dressmakers or, to use the grander term, mantua-makers. A mantua was a woman's cloak and the name first appears about 1850. It was customary for dressmakers, and tailors too, to move into a household and spend several weeks with the family making clothes. In 1851 the Rectory had a visiting dressmaker from Pembrokeshire who would probably have been recommended to Mrs Evans, the Rector's wife, who also came from there. Sally, daughter of 'Thomas Drefach', did twelve days needlework at 3d a day in 1843 at Morfa Gwyn: a frock for Sarah Evans cost seven pence halfpenny and a shirt nine pence. Poor women often worked as laundresses; if a woman was widowed, her neighbours would sometimes club together to buy her a mangle to do this work on a professional basis.

Of the nine shoemakers and cobblers finding employment in New Quay at this time, some had come from Llandysul and Newcastle Emlyn, reinforcing the impression that craftsmen were attracted there because New Quay offered better prospects of employment. Thomas Jones in Rock Street charged 5/- for making a pair of girl's shoes and 7/6 for men's shoes; soleing alone cost 1s.4d in the 1840s. Thomas and Judith, his wife, were members of Tabernacle Chapel and their sons, the Revs William Jenkin Jones, and Evan, born in 1838, were missionaries in Brittany for some twenty-five years.

Shops here varied from the big grocer's and draper's shops kept by the Timothys to little ones scarcely to be dignified by that name, described by Mrs Myra Evans in Atgofion Cei Newydd. "In the window of the cottage there would be just a currant cake and a stone bottle. The shop itself was in the kitchen and all there would be for sale were one or two jars of jam and some biscuits."(10) Several widows set up as bakers or confectioners to support their families. Margaret Davies had her shop at 8 Pen-y-wig in 1851; she was the widow of John Davies, a carpenter, and possibly it was her husband's workshop that gave the name Carpenter's Lane or Land to the path going down the back of Penwig to Church Street, emerging by the old cottage called Renown, named after a Swansea schooner. Margaret's son, Thomas, was apprenticed to a sail-maker, John, aged 10, was a scholar. At No 6 Pen-y-wig, Mary Davies also baked to support her three little daughters and at 11 Pen-y-wig Row Mary Thomas did sufficiently well from her "confectionary" to support five year old Eliza and two year old Margaret and keep a servant, Mary Davies, to look after them. Another Mary Davies had a bakery at 6 'Dole' Row, her son David was only a year old. Two older widows baked at Pengeulan: 71 year old Esther Davies at the former public-house, the Crown, at 15 Pengeulan and at No 20 Anne Davies carried on a similar business. Locally made sweets continued to be popular in the early part of this century and my father and his brothers bought "loshins" at a little cottage shop in Rectory Square. Another favourite was "cosin caws", round sugar balls, pink and yellow, sold from stalls at New Quay Fair on 12th November. This fair was held from the 1820s at least and in its heyday stalls stretched from the Black Lion down the Front and up Church Street. It may seem surprising that so many bakers could flourish here at one time but it must be remembered that at this period an oven was a comparative rarity in a cottage and most of the cooking was done over an open fire.(11) As late as the first decade of the 20th century, after the blacksmith Owen Davies' death, his spinster sisters supported themselves in this way at the Efail Fawr.

Many women ran public-houses here. At one time or another New Quay has had twenty-four 'pubs'. This is apt to give the misleading impression that it was like a Wild West town, full of saloons. It was comparatively easy to set up in business in a public-house: a licence had to be applied for at the Quarter Sessions but this could cost as little as 4/-. Most farms brewed their own beer so the average person would have learnt to do so at some time in their lives. However a study of the Censuses reveals that not all the pubs were active at the same time although the old names lingered on as long as the cottages existed. One of the oldest was the Blue Lion mentioned earlier. In 1841 it was not operating as a pub but was occupied partly by a tinman named John Griffith and his son who made kitchen and farm utensils and partly by Owen Owens, the blockmaker, a convenient site for his work on the ships. However, in the 1820s and 1830s it had still been a pub, run by John

New Quay Fair Day 1908, photographed in Church Street, a stall can be seen further down the street, behind the children. Author's collection.

Phillips, who bought the malt from which he brewed his beer from John Evans, Morfa Gwyn's malt-house at gyngolau. A bushel of malt cost 8/6 in August 1829 and had risen by a shilling in October. Jane the barmaid was often detailed to fetch the malt and John Phillips seems to have taken about six or eight bushels a month. John Evans recorded that he celebrated New Quay Fair Day there with 8d worth of ale in 1829. The Union public-house was also at Tangeulan.

Other early pubs included the Angel, the Blue Bell, the Ship, the Crown, the White Hart and the Penywig all on Pengeulan or near the Front, but only the Crown and the Penywig were operating in 1841, the former run by Esther Davies and the latter by Catherine Evans, then aged 72, and both had retired by 1851. However the Crown and the Blue Bell were re-opened as pubs later in the century. The Dolau was kept by Elinor Evans and is probably the only pub with a continuous history, still flourishing today. John Phillips of the Blue Lion had moved to Rock Street, then known simply as the Terrace and opened another pub there. It is not named in the Census but was perhaps the Neuadd Rock, as an Ann Phillips was running it in 1881. It was probably opened up to serve the men working at the Quarry, for whom it was very convenient, only a short distance from their work. Another pub was opened later in Rock Street, called the Neuadd Arms (Mindraeth today) and was also operating in 1881. Both were named in honour of Neuadd farm on whose land they stood.

The Shipwright's Arms at Traethgwyn, though retaining its old name, was not a pub at the time of the Censuses from 1841. There was also the Red Lion at Traethgwyn, which provided lodgings in 1851. Though I was misled in being told stories of a pub at Cwnc-y-lili in the lifetime of Edward Warren Jones, who died in 1829, it did not, in fact, open until long after his death and first appears in the Census of 1871. It occupied a prime site after the long haul up from Llanina and just before the steep road to Cross Inn, so it was a convenient place for the men carting goods to rest their horses and wet their whistles. The oldest inn in the district was probably the Salutation in Gilfachreda, the name giving a clue to its origins, since it is supposed to commemorate the Biblical story of the Virgin Mary meeting her cousin Elizabeth and therefore must date from the Middle Ages.

The Black Lion was probably the earliest hostelry in the village and certainly was always an Inn offering accommodation rather than simply a public-house. It was run for well over a hundred years by the same family, beginning with John Patrick, who came to New Quay from Lincolnshire in the 1830s.

Other pubs which flourished in the mid-nineteenth century were the Star in lower Church Street, run by Joseph Davies from Troed-yr-aur; in 1844, an indefatigable walker who had covered the 19 miles from Cardigan that day had tea there for 9d.(12) the Farmers' Arms in Farmers' Row, later High Street, was run in 1851 by John Davies, from Llannarth; James Davies, the former Harbour Master, opened the Ship on Launch, now named Pennard, in Church Street, sometime in the late 1840s. In 1851, the Castle was built halfway up Church Street on the corner of Mason Square, by John Davies, a retired farmer of Gwaun-yr-efail, Cross Inn, first cousin of the Neuadd family who leased him the site. After his death in 1864, his widow Jane continued to run it until the 1870s, when she retired to live with her daughter and son-in-law at Arthach farm, Llandysuliogogo. By 1881 it was a grocer's shop. By then the Queen's Hotel had been built at the top of Church Street, by David Davies, to cater for the increasing number of summer visitors coming to New Quay. Another pub, the Ivy Bush, was opened in Church Street, opposite the Ship on Launch, a hair-dresser's today, run by Mrs Eliza Olsen, whose family came originally from Norway on sailing vessels. There was also the Wellington, opened probably soon after the eponymous general's great victory at Waterloo, and still an attractive cottage pub in my youth though now handsomely rebuilt and extended.

The White Lion must have been one of the first buildings in Park Street in the late fifties but its active life was quite short and it had closed before 1881. Nearby was the Commercial Inn owned by Jenny Phillips in 1870. She was the daughter of Evan Evans of Scubor Fawr, Llwyndafydd, where Henry VII stayed in 1485. In 1852 she married John Evans the younger of Morfa Gwyn and they had three children. After his early death, she married Jenkin Phillips, Master Mariner of New Quay in 1863 and on his death she married Griffith Thomas, joiner, of 'Starfach' in 1876. It is not quite clear whether the Commercial Inn of 1870 mentioned in Jenny's family papers, (13) is the same as the Sailors' Arms of 1871, operated by Mary Williams. Certainly that was later known as the Commercial Hotel, which suggests that the two amalgamated as they were very close, the former being where the Football Club now is, and the latter being on the corner of what is now Uplands Square.

The proprietors Evan and Margaretta Jones with their eldest daughter outside the Queen's Hotel. They subsequently moved to Esgair House and for many years thereafter the Hotel was run by the Edwards' family. Courtesy of Mrs Dorothy Harding. The carriage provided an important service to visitors, fetching them from the railway station at Llandysul.

Today it is known as the Seahorse. Park Street acquired its name because earlier a cottage called Parc, belonging to Towyn Farm, existed there.

In George Street, the Prince of Wales was opened in the 1870s by John Davies "Innkeeper and fisherman" and flourished for over sixty years; more short-lived was the Belle Vue near the group of houses known as the Arba, opened when they were built after 1868 and operating till the 1880s. Finally, the Penrhiwllan Inn was open by 1881, run by Abraham Davies, innkeeper and carrier, and is still a pub today. The carriers were important personalities in the parish, until the buses came in 1907. They provided a combined public transport and delivery service. Three of the earliest known carriers were Thomas Jones of Pant-y-gwartheg, Joshua Davies, Penllaincefn and Daniel Jones of Blaen-y-waun, who were working in the 1840s and after. A contemporary of Abraham Davies was William Thomas, son of William Thomas, clog maker of 4 Brongwyn Street, New Quay's last carrier. William Thomas began carrying passengers to Llandysul on 30th April 1878 and continued the service for precisely twenty-nine years, retiring on 30th April, 1907, when the introduction of the Great Western railway bus service made his own service unprofitable. In a good year he earned about £250, August being one of the best months, when he would earn about £37. The winter months were naturally the poorest for passengers and in February takings seldom amounted to more than £10. Besides passengers, he carried goods of all kinds and executed a multitude of commissions for New Quay people, keeping a meticulous record. (14). His lively conversation whiled away the journeys very pleasantly for his passengers, something very much missed when the service was replaced by buses.

Through the references in the Census one can also trace the development of the present layout of New Quay and the sketch-map (Plate 12) indicates the dates on which respective streets were built. The opening up of a road to the quarry for the tramway carrying stones to build the pier, soon led to it being lined with new houses: the two halves of the long terrace being known as North Terrace and Rock Street; today houses at the far end of the street are still known as North End. The Tithe Map of 1847 (15) shows that New Quay still only covered half the area it did in the 20th century. Church Street had been rapidly built up to at least halfway up the hill and a few houses had been built above Rock street in Mariner's Row and were mostly occupied by sea captains, as the name suggests; Farmers' Row was built at the same time, connecting it with Church Street. All this area belonged to Neuadd farm and when Evan Evans, Neuadd, died in 1844, he bequeathed it between his daughters Margaret and Martha. Martha married Captain Griffith Jones, master of the Syren, and they built Prospect house on the corner of Rock Street, to live in after their marriage. Their daughter, Mary, inherited this part of the estate and upon her death in 1945 it was sold to the tenants, it included 1-12 Rock Street, Nos 25-31 as well as the Wellington Inn and Wellington place, Albion House and Esgair House in Mason Square. The prices then for the individual houses in Rock Street ranged from £210 to £500 and Prospect House sold for £2,000. The Albion, a draper's shop and house, went for £900 and Esgair House for £500. The Wellington Inn was purchased for £900.

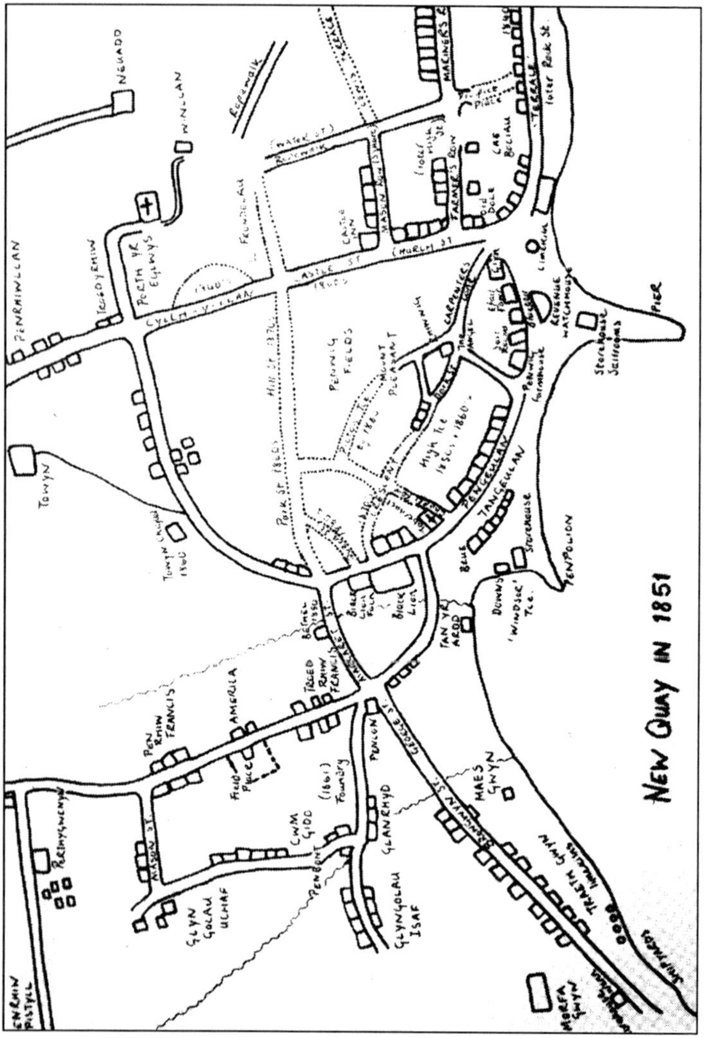

Plan of New Quay in 1851 with dotted lines representing streets as they were built later.

Church Street was named appropriately as it led up towards the parish church, but the building of the Castle pub opposite the Albion in 1851 led to the rest of the street being known briefly as Castle Street as it developed over the next few years; it was completed by the late 1870s, by which time Lewis Terrace was also built, which commemorated Lewis Lewis one of the original purchasers of the Neuadd Estate. High Terrace, begun in the 1840s, was completed about twenty years later, culminating in Gomer Crescent. Picton Terrace was built in the 1870s. Some of the houses there were specifically for the Coastguards and they had a commanding view of the Bay. By then the Coastguards formed a Naval Reserve and were required to perform military drill as well as training for coastal defence. Many were called up in the Crimean War in the 1850s. A cliff lookout was built on top of Pengraig. My grandmother, born in 1865, recorded in a school essay in 1880, the smartness of the coastguards' drill: perhaps this was in anticipation of the impending inspection by the Duke of Edinburgh, Prince Alfred, second son of Queen Victoria, who was Admiral Superintendent of the Naval Reserves between November 1879 and November 1882, when he visited New Quay.

Hill Street may have been begun in the late 1870s but, according to my Aunt Phyllis, who grew up there, she was born in Water Street in the first decade of the 20th century, because their new house in Hill Street wasn't finished. Theirs was Bronallt not far from the foot of Hill Street, so it was not completed until a few years before 1914.

The Coastguard Lookout on top of Pengraig, before 1914. Courtesy of Mrs P Cosmo-Jones.

All these houses were built of stone as opposed to the earlier clom cottages, and there was plenty of work for the masons. Mason Square (now re-named by the Council Stryd yr Hen Goleg to commemorate the nearby Tutorial School) was half-way up Church Street as the 1851 Census clearly shows, and not at the top of Water Street, according to another recent Council sign. Mason Square it always was to the children growing up in adjacent Lewis Terrace. It must not, either, be confused with Mason Row, up between Glyngolau and Perth-y-gwenyn Mason Square derived its name from the Reeses who lived there for most of the 19th and into the 20th century, a family of five masons. John Rees, the elder, had come to New Quay from Llandysuliogogo before 1833 and his four sons Isaac, John, Daniel and Owen were all employed with him. John Rees the younger, who built Towyn chapel in 1861 was a very talented man. Evan Joshua James, later Town Clerk of New Quay, wrote of his "genius" as a monumental mason, that he came from a family of noted athletes and was a skilled musician.(16) He taught generations of Towyn children tonic solfa and was the conductor of the New Quay choir for many years, walking with it to attend neighbouring Eisteddfodau, in Nanternis for example. Ap Cei Newydd recalled attending Eisteddfodau at Llanybydder and more locally again at Cefn Gwyddil farm when the New Quay choir won, singing Joseph Parry's "Gweddi Gwraig y Meddwyn". John Rees also played a prominent role in the early Regattas, first held in 1874. "There was one landlubber at the helm of one of the big boats at the Regatta for many years and that was Mr John Rees...he had a great reputation as a tactician in a boat race." The first Regatta took place on a fine sunny day in the presence of a huge crowd from far and near. "The principal event was the sailing race. In that race was the Nanta, the Luna (which belonged to Mr John Evans, chemist, Penwig and owner of half New Quay) and other big boats and there was also a very small boat called The Saucy Jack, belonging to an ex-coastguardman. As it happened on that day the breeze was faint and the bigger boats made very slow progress so the little Saucy Jack was an easy first." Sports of all kinds were also held, including negotiating the greasy pole, set up in Cae Blociau, to get a leg of mutton. Ap Cei Newydd was very proud of his friend William Jones, the future missionary to Brittany, who, when no-one achieved the summit of the pole won a footrace for the prize, starting from Pen-yr-Odyn above the limekiln on Dolau Beach, to the Quarry and back. (17)

John Rees was also a skilled fisherman. In the autumn and winter he regularly went fishing for herrings. He did not have his own boat, but like many other people he had nets which were lent to a boat and a share of the catch given in return. There were only three fulltime fishermen in New Quay in the Census of 1851: fishing continued to be a part-time occupation for many as it had been for centuries. The three were Phillip Phillips, Shipwright's Arms, aged 63, and as one might expect, born in the parish; David Davies, 2 Towyn Cottages, born in Llannarth and living with his sisters, Sara and Elizabeth, both born in New Quay; and the husband of Esther Evans who lived at 2 Glyngolau and who was absent at the time. They caught "soles, oysters and turbot" according to Samuel Lewis whose Topographical Dictionary of Wales (1833) extolled the local "Fish of very superior quality". In later years large fishing fleets from ports in the North of England came to New Quay, attracted by the plentiful shoals.

Two other masons lived in Brongwyn Street and had wonderfully Biblical names: Methusalem David and his grandson Abraham. They and a Thomas Davies did a good deal of work for John Evans, Morfa Gwyn. In 1834 Thomas Davies was paid £11/18/6 for building a barn, cart-house, stable and cowshed at Morfa Gwyn. In 1836 he was paid £2/12/6 for "finishing the walls and slating William Davy's house at Traethgwin"; Abraham, when building a new house at Traethgwyn, was paid 1/3 a perch (sixteen and a half feet).

In the late 1850s, David Evans, the eldest son of Neuadd farm, who was a timber merchant, built himself the big house known as Frondolau, as his mother still farmed Neuadd, at the top of Water Street, which was built a little later. Water Street was named for the little stream, Pistyll Bach, which emerges as a spring in Ivy Place and, so it was said, was used to wash the lead ore from the mine inherited by David. Rather surprisingly no miners are listed in the Census at any time though there are references to a few quarrymen including David Isaac of Pwllglas and Evan Evans from Cardigan. Evan Evans, Neuadd, refers to the lead as "recently discovered" in his will, proved 1844, but it cannot have been a useful vein of ore and probably not worth working for long.

George Street and Francis Street grew up in the 1840s and in the 1860s Margaret Street, named like them for members of the Francis family of Carmarthen who owned the land on which all three streets were built: they became a well-known firm of estate agents in the 20th century. At first, Francis Street, because of its length and steepness, was known as Penrhiw Francis and Troedrhiw Francis. As was the case elsewhere in New Quay, the cottages and houses there were let on sixty-year leases. The estate was sold in 1923 enabling the tenants to buy their own homes. The 18 acre farm of "Zoar" went for £835; and "Clyngoleu Fields together with Sites of Old Farm House and Bragty Old Cottage" (the Malt-house once owned by John Evans, Morfa Gwyn), went for £350. The freehold shop and the ruins of two cottages which had recently burnt down in Pilot Place were sold for £100. "Prior to the fire this whole property was let at the annual rent of £6/16/0d". Two Freehold Cottages known as "Lower and Middle House", Francis Street, with a bake-house and garden plots, went for £70. And Manchester House, Gardens, Outbuildings and Land" were sold to the tenant Dr Walter T James, for £650. Manchester House was a shop, built on part of what had been, sixty years before, Brookfield House with seven acres of land, tenanted by Elizabeth Timothy, widow of Evan. The name Brookfield was subsequently translated as Ty Nant, the name the property still bears.

Apparently the last street to be erected in New Quay was Queen Street, built on land originally known as Parkllwyd., the houses were built in its garden in the 1880s and the street probably so named to mark Queen Victoria's Golden Jubilee. At one time Parkllwyd was occupied by Dr John Jones, and was owned by the Timothys, who subsequently built Rose Hill on the site. Dr Jones gave over forty years service to the town. Like so many others he was attracted to the place in the 1830s, from his native parish of Penboyr, Carmarthenshire. He was not, however, the earliest known doctor here: Joseph Davies, surgeon, was living here in 1811 at Penrhiw. He went so far as to christen one of his sons Aesculapius, after the ancient Greek doctor and another was named Horatio for the hero of the day, Lord Nelson.

Street names are mentioned in all the Censuses but house names were a much later development, appearing for the first time in the 1871 Census: hitherto the enumerator had merely numbered houses from their starting-point though some groups of cottages had names derived from their location: Penlon at the cross-roads above Pilot Place; Penbont on the way up to Pentrecagal (now Pentregarth) where there was and is a little stream, Nant Ifan; Frontowyn, near Towyn Farm; Black Lion fach near the Hotel, and Tan-yr-ardd for the cottages below the Black Lion. Some old names still persisted: Dark Lane for the road linking High Terrace and the Front, though it was later changed to the pleasanter-sounding White Street, it was also briefly named Widow Street as so many lived there. South John Street replaced Pen-y-wig Row, and denoted the houses on the Front and "around the Horn" as the windy corner of the Blue Bell was nicknamed.

The most recent developments have been the trim Council Houses built in the post-war years, between Frondolau and the Church and appropriately named Cylch-y-llan. These provided homes for young New Quay families as well as re-housing some of the cottage dwellers. A few new houses have extended Lewis Terrace up the cliff and others have taken advantage of the superb viewpoints on Penrhiwpistyll hill. More houses have been built on Towyn land, opposite the Penrhiwllan Inn and a large new estate was built at the Arba and named Cwm Halen, after the parish's boundary stream which runs alongside, but basically New Quay's lay-out has remained unaltered for a hundred years and more.

Throughout this period of prosperity and after the decline of New Quay as a busy port with the consequent decline of the ancillary trades, the farms continued to employ a good many people as they had for centuries: on each one there were at least four or five servants, male and female, in permanent employment. At Neuadd, the largest farm in New Quay, of 140 acres, Elizabeth Evans who continued to farm it after her husband's death in 1844 till her own death in 1870, employed two labourers and had three farm servants who "lived-in": David Rees aged 32 from Llandysuliogogo, John Davies aged 20 and Thomas Lloyd, aged 18, both from Llanina, in 1851. Her two house servants were Elizabeth Davies, 20, from Llandysuliogogo and Charlotte Evans from Cytblwyf, aged 17, named probably for her parents' landlord's sister, Charlotte Longcroft. A good many girls went into domestic service. In 1851 thirty-one women and girls were so employed, many in their early teens. The youngest farm employee mentioned in the 1851 Census was Margaret Davies from Llannarth, aged 8, who worked as a shepherdess at Frongoch Farm, Llanllwchaearn, though like Little Boy Blue she would have been more of a herder than a shepherd. Besides the men and women permanently employed on the farms, The Report on the Employment of Women and Children

Potato Picking at Cefngwyddil Farm (which dates from at least the 16th century), in about 1930. Apart from the clothes, this photograph could have been taken any time in the previous 100 years or more. Horses were still being used to transport the crop and the traditional baskets were provided for gathering the potatoes, and can be seen on the right of the photograph.

in Agriculture in 1867 suggests that many were employed seasonally between April and November. There are many comments in contemporary school log books from 1860 onwards relating to these absences, the child returning to the school in the winter. Even in the 1940s and 1950s, the October half-term holiday was known as Potato Week and many children still worked on farms, picking potatoes.

Detailed accounts of servants' wages are available in the Morfa Gwyn papers: in 1835 David Jones was hired for the year at £5/10/- with his wages advanced to him as required and the residue paid at the end of the year:

Febry 8	Cash to pay his brother for wach (sic)	10/-
March 17	Cash to get tobacco	6d
April 4	" " " "	6d
" 22	" " " "	1/0
May 20	" " " "	7d
June 7	" " " "	6d
	Cash in fair Llanarth	1/0
June 29	Cash at Aberystwyth	4/0
July 15	Cash to get tobacco	1/0
26	Cash to pay Daniel Jones tailor	1/0
	Cash to his brother to pay for cloth	4/0
Aug 26	Cash to get tobacco	1/0
Sept 2	" " " "	1/0
14	" " " "	7d
22	" at fair Llanarth	1/0

Oct 1 Cash to get tobacco 6d

17 " " " "

7d

November Cash at New Quay Fair 2/6

For Isaac tailor making clothes 4/0

£1/15/3

Wages for the year £5/10/-

David loosing (sic) 1and a half weeks 3/1and a halfpenny

£5/6/10 and a halfpenny

By cash at sundry times £1/15/3
When settling £3/11/7 and a halfpenny £5/6/10 and a halfpenny

In 1843 Owen Parry was hired at £5/4/- plus enough ground to set one bushel of potatoes, a fairly common arrangement. The servant would work on this patch himself and could sell or dispose of the produce as he liked. Like David, Owen received money throughout the year to buy tobacco and attend fairs; and in addition, on two occasions, cash to go to "Panteg wedding" and to "Llangrannog wedding" and stockings which cost 2/-. At the end of the year the actual cash he received was £2/3/7 halfpenny. These servants who lived in would also have full board. Farmers' diet altered little at this time and remained the same into this century, revolving chiefly around bacon and potatoes. Flummery too was often eaten for breakfast or supper, in summer, known as uwd sucan in South Wales, a kind of jellified porridge, eaten cold and often served to workers at mid-day during the hay harvest. Cawl (broth) was the dish most commonly served in winter but Cawl Awst when many fresh vegetables were available in August was considered the best. In New Quay, according to S Minwel Tibbott's Welsh Fare, a feast known as Cawl Awst was held primarily for sailors on New Quay beach on the first day of August. The broth was boiled over a fire on the beach in a large cauldron and everyone would contribute some food.

Other farm workers were employed on a casual basis and were paid for specific tasks, but although they did not receive an annual wage they could count on regular work. For instance John Evans, Morfa Gwyn, employed John James Tirffynnon and his wife Sarah on a variety of farm work between 1836 and 1843. Below are typical extracts from the account books:

1836 John James, Tyrffynon (sic)		
	4 days at the garden	2/4
	2 days Kiln drying corn	1/2
	Five and a half perches stone hedge at 2/- a perch	10/6
1841	Mending hedges in Park	
	Maespwll 10 and a half perch at 5d (per perch)	
	Cae Berth 24 perch at 3d	
	Cae Gwastod 14 perch at 4d	
1842 2	days cutting willows Feb with wife Sarah	
1843 May	David thrashing half day	6d
July	Thomas Troedyrhiw digging between potatoes	
	One and a quarter days	1/3
Oct	John and Sarah reeping rhy grass (sic)	1/10 and a halfpenny

	John and Sarah harvesting	6/6		
1844 May 8	David half day thrashing barley			6d
25	David half day thrashing wheat		1/-	
1845 Jan 14	David killing and cutting swain (sic)	1/-		
April	David killing pig		1/-	
	David one day setting licks (sic) in garden	1/-		

In Atgofion Ruth Mynachlog, Ruth Jones, born on Banc Sion Cwilt in 1856, recalls going to Cruclas Farm as a child of 8 to mind cattle as they grazed on the then unfenced moor. She was paid a halfpenny a day and her keep. In later years, when at 13 she was "too old to herd and not strong enough to be a maidservant" she returned home to help on the family's small-holding, but still worked on a casual basis at harvest time. She recalls going with several others with their sickles "as an advertisement" to Aberystwyth and being hired to harvest on farms in the Borth area, for 2/- a day and her keep. That was in 1875. She travelled there in Jenkin Thomas's cart and worked there for two weeks before returning home. (18)

Although the more skilled jobs like laying hedges and building walls were carried out by men, it will be observed that women also worked on labouring jobs as they had when the pier was being built and as they would on the Patent Slip in the 1860s. (qv) Besides Sarah James, John Evans also recorded payments to Thomas Drefach's daughter Catherine, in November 1843, when he paid her a shilling for digging potatoes for two days. She was probably quite young, sister of the Sally who made dresses and shirts for the family at Morfa Gwyn.

Drefach was then one of the cottages along Brongwyn Street.

Benjamin Jones the miller, formerly at Llanina Mill, which had ceased work at this date, (see my recent Llanina & Cytblwyf, 2011) also did some work for John. He was paid for half a day's harvesting in 1845 and also cut drains in Cae Berth Uchaf.

Besides the mill at Llanina, and Wern Mill Gilfachreda, both watermills, there had been a windmill at Llain-yr-orfa at the top of the steep hill leading from New Quay to Maen-y-groes. It was operating in the 1830s as it was marked on the 1834 OS map but it had ceased operations by 1841 and was dismantled by Evan Evans, millwright, who was then living at Maen-y-groes. Parts of it were used when he built Melin Bompren on the Soden River, which worked till 1957 and after its closure was removed to St Fagan's Folk Museum.(19) A millwright's is generally an itinerant job: he was a highly skilled craftsman who built and serviced mills.(20) Other mills in the vicinity were Nant-y-pelau mill, also in the Soden valley, at Nanternis, one at Llwyndafydd, one at Cwm Tudu, one in Synod Inn and Llannarth.

Llanina Mansion and its estate gave employment to many local people. In 1851, the family were not in residence at the time of the Census, but present then was Thomas Richards, described as Steward of the estate, farming 200 acres and employing 7 labourers, two of whom lived on the premises and there were 3 house servants. They also had a coachman, Henry

Wilcox from Pembrokeshire. In 1871, when the Longcrofts were in residence, they were employing 13 people: a butler, whose family had a cottage nearby, with the unusual surname of Erasmus; a coachman, a stable-boy, the then farm bailiff, Evan Thomas, two ploughmen, a housekeeper, a ladies' maid, housemaid, kitchen maid and dairy-maid, a gamekeeper and his assistant.

Charles Richard Longcroft, who inherited the Llanina estate and lands in Pembrokeshire and Carmarthenshire with his sister Charlotte, who married Thomas Lloyd of Coedmor, from Edward Warren Jones, their godfather, who died in 1829, was High Sheriff of Cardiganshire in 1834 and a director of the New Quay Harbour Company, as mentioned above. He died in 1888 and was succeeded by his son Charles Edward Longcroft, 1842-1892. He married Catherine Alicia, daughter of the Rev E Holcombe and they had two sons and two daughters. The elder son was Charles Alexander Holcombe Longcroft, born 1883, who served in World War I and became an Air Vice-Marshall; the younger son Edward Francis, born in 1885, and also served in World War I, he died 30th November 1914; the daughters were Edith and Gwendoline. The latter was closely involved with New Quay for many years, riding side-saddle every day during the first World War over to the village to supervise the ladies' allotments as part of her contribution to the war effort, and stabling her horse at the Black Lion.(21) Until the family severed their links with the mansion between the wars, they continued to fill the traditional role of lords of the manor.

Old occupations survived alongside more modern ones. As everyone knows, Sir Robert Peel introduced the first police force in 1829, with the result that the first constables were known as 'peelers' or 'bobbies', the latter a name which has survived until today. Within a few years of their creation, New Quay also had its own policemen, although the police station was not erected until the 20th century. These new constables replaced the old parish constables who had been elected annually by the historic Manorial Court, dating from the 14th century, which had been held in the Manor of Caerwedros, encompassing New Quay, up until the 1830s. Only a few of its records survive at the National Archives at Kew, but they reveal that one 'petty constable' was elected for each parish. Their duties had been closely associated with the parish vestry and they carried out its instructions, escorting malefactors to Cardigan gaol and 'alien' paupers to their place of settlement. It was very much a part-time occupation but equally unpopular for its intrusion into the customary daily round of those elected.(22) Among the earliest modern policemen assigned to New Quay were John Rees from Maenordeifi, who lodged with his wife at 3, North Terrace and a Mr Nicholas, who lived at Traethgwyn and may have come from Yorkshire, like his wife Jane, who alone was present when the enumerator called. This suggests that, like the Coastguard, the police were deliberately appointed from other districts. A third constable was Thomas Vaughan, from Pembroke, who lodged at the Red Lion.

As New Quay became more sophisticated, chemists, a bookbinder, photographers (23) and watchmakers made their appearance in later Censuses. By 1861, there were two resident clock-makers: Thomas Webb from Cardigan, in Rock Street and David Evans from Cribyn in High Street (formerly Farmers' Row). In 1857, Thomas Webb made a grandfather clock, commissioned as a wedding present for Owen Davies, the blacksmith, and his wife Elizabeth, daughter of the Castle Inn, with a blacksmith striking the hours on his anvil. Among other ingenious clocks he produced which can still be seen in New Quay, were ones with a rocking sailing ship, ticking away the time, and a lion which moved its eyes. One of the watchmakers, who lived in Mason Square, was known as "Genuine Job", from his fondness for the phrase when describing his own work. The Welsh have always had a talent for bestowing appropriate and amusing nicknames and New Quay was no exception: there was Dai Bara Te from his habit of dipping his bread and butter into his tea; and Dai Come Back - after he and his wife had a tiff he left a note saying simply "Gone away"; he thought better of it after a few days and sent her a telegram saying simply "Dai come back". Most nicknames, however, were associated with the ships connected with their families. These nicknames were essential in a society where Christian names seldom left a familiar and narrow range or surnames either. Rather astonishingly, even for Wales, three surnames alone accounted for 164 families, well over half the population in 1851. Seven surnames in all covered seven-eighths of the population: in order of frequency they were Davies, Evans, Jones, Thomas, Williams, Phillips and Rees. Most girls in New Quay were christened Mary or Margaret with Anne and Elizabeth also high in the popularity stakes and the majority of men were named

David, John or Evan. There were a fair number of Biblical Christian names too: Abraham, Benjamin, Daniel, Enoch, Isaac, Job, Samuel and Solomon; Sarah, Hannah and Magdalen as well as an occasional Ruth and Deborah. Despite the growth of the village there was little variation in names throughout the 19th century.

CHAPTER V

Education, Religion and Politics

New Quay's prosperity was also reflected in an increasing concern with education. Reading the Bible had been taught in the Rev Griffith Jones' Llanddowror's circulating schools in the 18th century, but they were held here only intermittently, although they reached many people, 109 at the last school held here in 1775. (1) Up until his death in 1763, the Rev John Pugh of Motygido, Llannarth had run a school for many years at his home where he taught farmers' and craftsmen's sons and a number of his students entered the Church. (2) A similar school was held at Castellhywel thereafter under the direction of David Davies. (3) We know that this was attended by David Peter, the future Nonconformist minister, after the death of his father, who had been working as a shipbuilder in New Quay. His biography mentions that he had previously had six years' schooling with Mr Evan Davies, Troedrhiw. Unfortunately Troedrhiw is a common place name. In 1810, the Rev Thomas Phillips had opened his famous Academy at Neuaddlwyd, near Aberaeron, and it flourished under his direction for thirty years. (3) For the first half of the 19th century, the majority of children probably attended only Sunday schools like that taught by George Parry at Penrhiwgaled, because they were free. However, there were, in 1824, two schoolmasters in the district, John Davies of Coed-y-brain, Cytblwyf, in the little township between Llanllwchaearn and Llanina, and David Davies of Parcllwyd, Cytblwyf. Their children were baptised at Penrhiwgaled, but it is likely that they kept a fulltime school as that is given as their profession, whereas George was a shop-keeper as well. The Rector of New Quay at this period, was an absentee, the Rev David Jenkins, (4) so the church was served only by a succession of curates. It was not until 1838 that New Quay had a resident Rector, the Rev David Evans, MA, formerly Headmaster of Cardigan Grammar School. Although married, he had no family and combined his parochial duties with teaching, and the commodious Rectory, when it was finally built by 1851 was used as a boarding house for a number of his pupils, others being lodged nearby. One pupil's home address was Peebles, Scotland, this was George Pringle, aged 10. The other scholars were older and their names suggest connections with old gentry families like the Steadmans and Tyglyn Aeron. The only local boy was Evan Davies, Llannarth, aged 18. It is probable, however, that the coaching establishment he ran, had only begun when he had the accommodation that the Rectory provided, (before that he had to rent a house, and lived at Penwig for a time), as his school isn't mentioned in 1846, when the government undertook an investigation into the state of education in Wales, in the wake of the unrest of the

Rebecca Riots, and their findings were published in a series of 'Blue Books' in 1847. From the severity of their strictures on the Welsh and their ignorant state, the survey was ever after referred to as "Brad y Llyfrau Gleision", the treachery of the Blue Books. There certainly appears to have been some bias among the commissioners, particularly against the survivors of Madam Bevan's charity schools, successors to those of the Rev Griffith Jones, which came in for a good deal of vitriolic comment. The extent of the criticism, however, depended on the attitude of the investigator. Henry Penry, whose task it was to report on New Quay, appears to have been very fair, compared with some of the other Assistant Commissioners.

In Llanllwchaearn he first visited the Calvinistic Methodist Sunday School on 6th December 1846 at Tabernacle. The Superintendent of the Sunday School was described as "a superannuated officer connected with this port, under the Government". This must have been George John, born at St David's, Pembrokeshire, who had been at New Quay more than twenty years and was a retired coastguard. Lodging in his house in 1851 was Edward Lewis aged 46, a schoolmaster from Llanfihangel Genau'r Glyn in North Cardiganshire, who may have assisted George in teaching at Tabernacle since Henry Penry mentions "an active and intelligent secretary". Henry Penry was extremely impressed by all the classes, which ranged from small boys, young men and women (taught separately) to "elderly men chiefly sailors"; all revealed a good understanding appropriate to their classes and a wealth of Scriptural knowledge.

The following day he walked up Francis Street to the old Wesleyan Methodist chapel between Soar and Perth-y-gwenyn, although Henry Penry describes it as "formerly known as Zion", it appears to have housed religious services until 1858 at least. Welsh Wesleyan Methodism began to penetrate to Cardiganshire around 1806, but the sect was never as popular as the Calvinistic Methodists or the Independents and by 1851 it only represented 6 percent of the population of Cardiganshire when 77.5 percent were Nonconformists: the Independents amounting to 22 percent and the Baptists 8 percent, so over half were Calvinistic Methodists. (6) In 1858 New Quay was part of the Wesleyan Lampeter-Cardigan circuit with chapels at Lampeter, Cardigan, Llandysul, Tregaron and Capel Ficer in Ffos-y-ffin. New Quay Wesleyans shared the services of the Rev Robert Owen who ministered there and often walked to Capel Ficer for Communion.

The school at the chapel was conducted by Thomas Evans, aged 40, from Aberarth, who lodged at Maen-y-groes with Mrs Mary Evans, who kept a shop. Mr Penry thought the chapel a well-lighted and suitable building. The master "appeared rather an intelligent man and had been engaged many years as a teacher, but he is paid so little for his labour that he seems to have lost his spirit and energy for the duties". The scholars spelt well but read English badly and appeared to have little understanding of what they read. Today this building has long been in ruins and overgrown but it continued as a school for many years and Thomas Lloyd Evans, despite Henry Penry's impression of weariness with his work, remained a teacher until his death in 1884. He is noted for the excellent way he taught navigation to many New Quay sailors.

Later the same day he visited Mr Evan Williams' school in Brongwyn Street. It was "recently built by Mr Williams, a well-lighted, dry and convenient building for a school." Mr Penry found that the children read extremely well and ventured to say he thought "they were superior to most of what I have heard in this County". Their grammar and writing too were better than the scholars in Thomas Evans' school. They were studying Pinnock's Catechism of Geography but "without maps, their knowledge is not very extensive..... The master is not wanting in ability, nor in the tact and good nature required to make an effective and successful teacher," Mr Penry concluded.

The main problem, in a monoglot society, would always be the difficulty of familiarising themselves with a new and alien language, since all lessons were conducted in English, but it must be remembered that it was by their own choice. Everyone who discusses education at this period is adamant that all the parents were greatly concerned that their children should have a good command of English "because it was the only way to get on." Certainly the future sea-captains required it: Theophilus Davies, whose Cargo Book will be quoted from later on, had obviously learnt English, but his spelling would not have satisfied the Commissioners.

The zeal for learning which was undoubtedly present in New Quay is reflected by the establishment of a Newspaper Reading Room in 1854, opened on the 2nd of February by Charles Longcroft, Esq, and the Rev David Evans, Rector of Llanllwchaearn. Two daily papers were taken and several weekly papers, according to Y Wasg, the Welsh newspaper which reported this event and was printed monthly in Aberystwyth. Y Wasg frequently reported New Quay news but was rather short-lived, covering only the years 1854 and 1855. The weekly newspapers may have included The Welshman or the Carmarthen Journal or even the Caernarfonshire & Denbighshire Herald which often carried Cardiganshire news, all fairly long-established papers. The daily papers must have been from England since no daily newspaper was published in Wales until 1861. The Welsh appetite for journals, however, was insatiable and in 1861 the Keeper of the Printed Books at the British Museum wrote in Knight's Penny Cyclopaedia: "In almost every country the periodical portion of its literature has now assumed an importance unknown to previous stages of its history, but in no country is it so predominant as in Wales."(7) I have already mentioned Y Diwygiwr and many of these magazines were printed by Nonconformist editors so were probably unlikely to find their way into a reading room under the auspices of the Established Church. But, judging from the many survivals in New Quay's attics, they were subscribed to faithfully for many years.

It is a reflection of the zeal for reading and reading on religious subjects in particular, that even young sailors spent their hard-earned money on Bibles and on books of biblical commentaries. There exists a Welsh New Testament, printed in 1862, and on the flyleaf is written: "Owen Richard Davies, his book, bought at Liverpool Dec 20th 1866 on board the Dreadnought of New Quay." The price was 1/9. Owen Richard Davies was a son of the Castle public-house at New Quay, born in 1847. He drowned on a voyage from Callao to Hull in

1869. This is only one of several such books he purchased and inscribed in his fine clear hand. One has now been given to the library at Ty Mawr, Bishop Morgan's home, to commemorate this zeal for religion which he did so much to foster in the hearts of the Welsh.

Owen Richard Davies and his contemporaries benefited from the criticisms voiced by the Blue Books, since, however undeserved they were felt to be at the time, they did at least provoke more concern for better education and led eventually to the establishment of the University College of Wales at Aberystwyth. The British School Society opened a new school at Tabernacle Chapel in 1851, the schoolmaster being a Mr John Roberts from Corris, who had assisted Mr Evan Williams at his school in Brongwyn Street. He was then a very able young man in his twenties and he taught at New Quay until his premature death in 1872 at the age of 45. The school eventually moved to a building near the present Memorial Hall. After Mr Roberts' death, his widow Eleanor ran a sewing school in Hill Street.

The Royal Commission was considering only schools which catered for the poor, reckoned to be a hotbed of sedition, not only because of the Rebecca Riots, but also because of the mass rallies then being held in favour of Chartism and demanding universal suffrage, one man, one vote. They were certainly uninterested in another school at this period which catered exclusively for girls, and was run by the daughters of the officer commanding the Coastguard, Joseph Fauriel Barrett. Selina and Emily Barrett, the two eldest daughters, who sound rather like characters from Jane Austen novels, described themselves as "Preceptresses in English, French, Geography, Use of the Globes, Music and Drawing", essential adjuncts to a young lady's education. It is probable that they were assisted by Mary Anne Nash, aged 21, daughter of William Nash, Chief Boatman of the Coastguard; her sister Isabella, aged 16, was a pupil at the school. Altogether some seven girls in New Quay between the ages of 13 and 18 attended this school - at a time when it was very unusual for boys and girls to receive an education beyond the ages of 14 or even 12, and probably they had some younger scholars as well.

In 1851 about 148 children are described in the Census as scholars, 97 of them boys, representing about half the boys of accepted school age then living in the village. Only 29 of these were over the age of 13, but a number of these older pupils came from outside New Quay and were being coached by the Rev David Evans at the Rectory. Fewer than a quarter of the girls of school age are listed as receiving an education, although the enumerator is not always accurate on this point. Statistics suggest that most children went to school between the ages of 8 and 12, both girls and boys; Anne Evans of Towyn farm was in fact described as "retired scholar" at the age of 12. Only a few boys attended school below the age of 8 and no girls. Nevertheless, where families could afford the penny a day per child, sons and daughters had equal opportunities for learning. John Mathias, a sail-maker, had four children in school simultaneously, both girls and boys.

Besides the Rev David Evans' coaching establishment, the British School and the Misses Barretts' school for Young Ladies in the 1850s, Mr Joshua Jones kept a school for a good many years at Glyn Square, along with his other activities as Secretary of the New Quay Mutual Ship Insurance Society and the Patent Slip. In 1855, Lieutenant Joseph Barrett retired and his family moved from New Quay, so the girls' school came to an end. Another was opened some ten years later by Miss Hannah Jeremy from Carmarthenshire at 6, Mariner's Row. Miss Jeremy was 50 in 1871 and is described in the Census as a Governess; Miss Gertrude Stephens, aged 23, was her partner and they had one boarder, Anne Beynon, from Llannarth. Ap Ceinewydd, who is the source of much of the information on New Quay schools, also mentions "Ysgol Price" kept in a private house in Marine Terrace, probably in the 1860s.

After John Roberts' death, Mr Thomas Lloyd took over as headmaster of the British School. The principle of compulsory education was introduced in 1870 and in 1878 the Government established the New Quay Board School. The British School closed and Mr Lloyd was invited to become headmaster of the new school which flourishes today as the New Quay Primary School, in the original building, extended, and extensively modernised within.

As the British School had catered for younger children, Mr Wallace James set up a school for older pupils adjoining Towyn Chapel, built between 1858 and 1861, and this was taken over in 1880 by Mr Charles Hughes, and became known as Towyn Grammar School. One of its most famous pupils was Thomas Jacob Thomas:

Sarnicol, to give him his bardic name, and fortunately he has left us a unique account of attending “Yr Ysgol ar Lan y Mor”. (7) Born 13th April, 1873 and dying 2nd December 1945, Sarnicol took the name of the little house where he was born on Banc Sion Cwilt as his pen-name. When he was 14 years old, after receiving his early education at Capel Cynon, he went to school at New Quay. He recalls how he and his father in their best clothes, fortified by calls at several pubs, walked down to New Quay and how enormously impressed he was by Mr Hughes' parlour, he had never seen a room so handsome. The house was Rhoslwyn in Church Street. “In came a man with a gentle face, quiet speech and narrow black beard, modest brown eyes and a wide forehead. He was smartly dressed in a reddish suit with a gold watch-chain and a medal hanging from it.” Despite his calling, Mr Hughes appeared to be a shy man and the slight stoop he had made him appear even more retiring. The school fees were 15/- a quarter and a lodging was found for the boy with two others from ‘upcountry’, from Nanternis and Pencader, at Glan-yr-afon Cottage near the Dolau Inn, with “Pegi Glan-yr-afon”. His lodgings would cost 18d a week with fire and light as required. He would of course walk home at weekends. So on a Monday morning in late May, the boy of fourteen set out early from his farmhouse home with a white bag on his back containing his food for the week: a loaf, some cheese, a piece of bacon and some butter. He had a shilling in his pocket from which he had to buy tea and sugar: three pence worth of tea and a pound of sugar for tuppence, from “Lisa London house”; also a copy-book, ink and perhaps a pencil, leaving him with one penny for “frivolities”.

Charles Hughes and Towyn Grammar School pupils in 1885. Author's collection.

"The school was very small, cuddled up against Towyn Chapel like a lamb with its mother, with about twelve long desks, old-fashioned ones and some two dozen boys, from thirteen year olds to sailors who had spent ten years at sea and two or three girls".

Mr Charles J Hughes was a Bachelor of Arts of London University and as Sarnicol reminds us it was no small achievement to be a graduate in those days, especially in a place as "disadvantaged" as New Quay. He was widely read and capable of teaching subjects as diverse as Hebrew and Navigation but his favourite subject was Mathematics and "in that he reached a standard much higher than even BA". He kept perfect discipline, there was scarcely a sound in the school and in the four years Sarnicol attended Towyn Grammar School he only saw the cane used once. Everyone studied on their own, going up to the Headmaster's desk only when they needed assistance. He concluded his tribute, which appeared first in the Western Mail, by saying how fortunate he was that chance brought him under the influence of such a man as Charles Hughes, and that there were many like him who would happily corroborate his panegyric since they owe their successful careers to Mr Hughes' teaching and encouragement. Charles Hughes became the first Headmaster of the new County School at Aberaeron in 1899 and remained there until he retired in 1917, dying in 1920 at the age of 69. He is buried in the graveyard at Maen-y-groes.

Although Mr Thomas refers to New Quay as "disadvantaged", which indeed it was educationally compared with more populous districts, one cannot help feeling that the village was very fortunate in the quality of its teachers, not only Charles Hughes, but also David Cletwrian Jones (1858-1931), who succeeded him in the field of secondary education in the village. David Jones was the son of Thomas and Jane Jones, Nantgwynfynydd-ganol, Llannarth. When he was five years old his family moved to Rhandir, Talgarreg. He was the eldest of the children and was employed on the farm though he had some education in the village and at the well-known school at Pontsian. This was Rhydowen Grammar School, founded by the Rev Thomas Thomas in 1847, and before such education was available in the village a number of New Quay sailors went there to study navigation to qualify for their certificates. (qv)

Once David had learnt to read, he taught himself to such good effect that he opened a school on the farm in the 'sied siaffo', the chaffing or winnowing shed. It was said that as many as one hundred children attended it though he was only seventeen himself when he began it. He adopted the name Cletwrian when he began to write poetry. Subsequently he had four years at Carmarthen Presbyterian College, from 1877 to 1881, and then a year at the University in Aberystwyth, before becoming a teacher in Weston-super-Mare, and eventually headmaster there. Later he founded a Tutorial school in Penarth. He brought his school to New Quay in 1900 and carried it on first at the Glyn and then in a building at the foot of Lewis Terrace, which was still referred to as the Tutorial School up to its accidental destruction by fire in 2009, although it had been a private house for many years. Its site has now been built over. An exotic touch was added by the presence of both Greek and

Spanish students who came there to learn English for Mr Jones was well-known for his ability to teach the language to foreigners. He lived in Rhandir, Church Street, which he named for his boyhood home. After his death the school was continued for girls only, by his daughter Dora, for a few more years. Mr Jones had very high standards and everyone who attended the school spoke well of the education received there. A number of students went on to University and others attained high positions in the professions.(8)

As part of the general 19th century "concern with the social welfare of the people" which had led to "the notorious enquiry into the state of education in Wales" ......"it seemed desirable to the government of Lord John Russell to ascertain the amount of accommodation available to them for religious worship, and the extent to which it was used. The government therefore decided to undertake a religious census in connection with the ordinary census to be held in 1851". (9) This was a unique inquiry as a similar undertaking was never again considered. All ministers, rectors and vicars were asked to record the number of sittings in their places of worship and the number who attended regularly. It was subsequently believed that this gave rise to a somewhat unfortunate spirit of emulation between the chapels and churches if not between different denominations. Certainly the church was in retreat at this time throughout Wales before the rising tide of Nonconformity and this was reflected in New Quay.

The Rev Thomas Rees, from Llandysuliogogo, had succeeded the Rev Daniel Thomas at Maen-y-groes,

Students of the Tutorial School in 1910, David Cletwrian Jones, the Headmaster, is in the centre of the photograph. Author's collection.

where he had been assisting him since 1840, having been a student at Neuaddlwyd. Maen-y-groes reported the largest attendance of the 43 Independent chapels in Cardiganshire, with 300 scholars, ie Sunday School children, attending in the morning, 500 people and 200 scholars in the afternoon and 370 people and 230 scholars in the evening. In his report Mr Rees added "at six o'clock we have many meetings held occasionally for divine worship at different places in the neighbourhood". David Williams, in his article on the Census, comments: "This is a remarkable attendance and certainly required some explanation for the chapel only had 294 sittings. The minister had evidently gone out into the highways and hedges and compelled them to come in". (10)

Despite Mr Williams's justifiable scepticism over the figures, it was in fact considered necessary to erect another Independent Chapel at Wern that same year and within less than ten years to build Towyn Chapel at New Quay for 291 adherents of Maen-y-groes, so Mr Rees's figures cannot have been so very far out.

The building of Wern Chapel had been one of Mr Daniel Thomas's pet projects, but he died before it could be carried out. Thomas Lewis Lloyd of Nantgwyllt, Radnorshire, who then still owned Wern Newydd land, although the estate would be sold within the next generation, was amenable and gave a 999 year lease of sufficient land. The chapel was erected under the guidance of Daniel Thomas's stepson, Abraham Thomas of Llwynonn Farm and his son, Enoch, David Thomas of Wern Mill, William Richards, Rhydalen farm, John and James Jones of Waun, John and James Jones of Oernant and David Jones, smith, of Gilfachreda. The first minister was Mr Evan Jones, who already had the chapel of Pencae under his care. His and his successors' tenure was brief until in 1859 the Rev Jenkin Prytherch became their minister and officiated there for nearly fifty years.

The new chapel at New Quay stood on land given by Captain Evans, Towyn farm, master of the Viscata. It was built at a cost of £1,398/15/2d, by, as already mentioned, the very talented mason, John Rees the younger, and was regarded as one of the prettiest chapels in Wales by the authors of the standard history of the Independent Chapels. (11) It was designed to seat 750 people, a testimony to its members' faith in the continuing growth of New Quay and people still living today can remember it filled to overflowing.

At the time of the Religious Census, Tabernacle was under the care of the Rev Evan Jones from Llangeitho, who also farmed at Llaingrog, which he took over on the death of Job Evans, brother of John, Morfa Gwyn. The chapel had been rebuilt and enlarged in 1837, and in 1851 was attended by 280 adults and 120 scholars on Sunday morning and by 300 adults and 118 scholars in the evening.

The Baptist Chapel at New Quay, Bethel, originated with a single-minded couple, who moved to New Quay in the 1830s. Evan Thomas, a nailer, was born in Llanybydder and his wife Elizabeth in Lampeter. Before coming to New Quay with their four children, they had been members of Aberduar Baptist Church. The nearest Baptist Chapel was at Llwyndafydd and they worshipped there but also held meetings at their home in Brongwyn Street until Bethel was built as the result of their efforts in 1849, though Evan Thomas did not live to see it, having died in 1846. Elizabeth lived to the age of 90, dying in 1896; her daughter Martha Nailer, as she was always known, died in 1912: such was the persistence of nicknames in the community although her father had then been dead for over sixty years. The Rev Thomas Griffiths, the minister at Llwyndafydd, took the first services. At the time of the Religious Census, 120 people attended the afternoon service at Bethel and 110 in the evenings. It closed recently and although the façade has been preserved, it now forms part of Costcutters supermarket.

The chapels were fervent supporters of missionary endeavours in the "foreign field". As far back as the 1820s, Penrhiwgaled Chapel had sent missionaries to Madagascar. (12) Reference has already been made to the missionaries to Brittany, the sons of Thomas James, the shoemaker, in Chapter IV. In 1854, Tabernacle Chapel collected donations to purchase 500 New Testaments to be sent to China: "Draw, draw yn China a thiroedd Japan, plant bach melynion sy'n byw, ...Neb i ddweud am Dduw, Iesu cofia'r plant..." a hundred years later this hymn was still sung in the chapels of my childhood. Great interest too was taken in the missions to India and I remember a visiting missionary from India who made a huge impression on the children as she was dressed in a sari and persuaded us to dress up and re-enact the different Indian castes.

The U'Larsing, built at Traethgwyn in 1864, was named for the first convert achieved by Welsh missionaries in the Khassia Hills in India. His photograph appears on the cover of Ar Fryniau'r Glaw, a historical novel by Merfyn Jones, but based on the letters of Mrs Mary Lewis, wife of the missionary the Rev William Lewis, and published by Christopher Davies, Swansea, in 1980. (This book won the Prose Medal at the Pontrhydfendigaid Eisteddfod in 1978) The full story of the missionaries' work in India can be read in the biography: Y Parchedig John Roberts DD, Khasia, by R J Williams, printed at Caernarfon by the Calvinistic Methodists. One man from New Quay who worked in the Khassia Hills for forty years was John Ceredig Evans, son of Captain John Evans, Ty Ceredig, High Terrace, born 4th March 1855. He joined the Rev John Roberts in 1887 in Cherra to take charge of the Teachers' School established by Mr Roberts, which was later moved to Shillong and also to preach in local churches. His son Penry was born there in 1895 and his first wife Nell died out there. Two years later he survived a serious earthquake, which devastated the settlement, but it was restored. Another New Quay missionary who worked with Mr Evans was the Rev William Williams, who died 22nd April 1892. He was the son of David and Elizabeth Williams, Fron-nant and their grave records his burial at Shillong, Assam, India. In his retirement, the Rev Ceredig Evans lived at New Quay and died there in 1936.

U'Larsing was also commemorated in a house of that name in Hill Street, though it has since been renamed. A few doors away is a house that still bears the name Fwambo, which also commemorates a missionary endeavour, in Africa. David Picton Jones, who named the house, was born in New Quay on 20th January 1860, the son of Elias and Elizabeth Jones. He was educated by John Roberts at the British School and after leaving school was apprenticed to a carpenter. When he was 14 years old, he was sent to work with his uncle in Liverpool (13) but after a few months there he became convinced he wanted to be a minister and he returned to complete his education at Towyn Grammar School and then at the Presbyterian College at Carmarthen. Then he applied to the Missionary Society in London, was accepted, and sent to central Africa. He sailed on 17th May 1882 and reached Tanganyika at the end of February 1883. He remained there four years and was very successful but the place was proving so unhealthy for white people that after a spell of home leave during which he married, he was sent to Fwambo between lake Nyasa and Tanganyika. Here again he was in his element, fulfilling the roles of doctor, carpenter, gardener and teacher, justice of the peace and minister of the gospel. In addition he produced a book: Outlines of Kimambwe Grammar to aid missionaries in learning the local language and to help the people themselves to become literate. He also translated hymns and part of the Gospels into Kimambwe. In 1894 he was sent to found a new missionary station at Kimbole, building a chapel and a school. Owing to sickness among his fellow workers, Mr Picton Jones was responsible for running the missionary station almost single-handed and when he was finally relieved, his health had completely broken down. He returned to Wales in 1896 and as soon as he had recovered he finished his translation of the new Testament and a Kimambwe-English dictionary, which took him five years. He returned for a short time to

Matabele Land but in 1903 he was forced to return home for good, becoming minister of Peniel Green Chapel, Llansamlet and retiring eventually to New Quay and the house he named Fwambo. (14).

This seems an appropriate point at which to mention that one of the best-known Welsh hymns was inspired by New Quay: "Rwy'n gweld o bell y dydd yn dod", by the Rev Watkin H Williams, Brynaman, Carmarthenshire, (1855-1905), known throughout Wales by his bardic name "Watcyn Wyn". He was a regular visitor to New Quay, staying at the Black Lion in a room overlooking the sea, and it was there, early one morning that, watching the day dawn, he wrote his hymn.

At this time, the ancient parish church had 130 attenders at morning service plus 30 scholars; in the afternoon, 60 and 10 scholars. The dilapidated church was totally rebuilt in 1865 and in 1871 a small "mission church", Holy Trinity, was erected at Cross Inn, two miles inland. The Rev David Evans died in 1870 after thirty-two years at New Quay and Holy Trinity was completed by his successor, the Rev James Griffiths. He was described by the Independent Minister the Rev Josiah Towyn Jones, later a Liberal MP, as "by far the best preacher in New Quay and there is a danger that many will leave the chapels for the church." Towyn Jones himself was considered an exceptionally eloquent preacher. There was inevitably a good deal of resentment against the established church on the part of Nonconformists, harking back to real persecution in the early days of Dissent and the fact that though they were not members of the church they were still expected to contribute to its upkeep. At this period there was a very strong movement to dis-establish the Church in Wales, i.e. put an end to its status as a State Church. The Rev Josiah Towyn Jones was one of its strongest advocates in later life.

He was born in New Quay on 26th December 1858 at the cottage known as Towynbach, son of John Jones, shoemaker, and Elizabeth his wife. His brothers, David and Lewis, went to sea and became Master Mariners: Captain David Jones, Rhianfa and Captain Lewis Jones, Waterloo. Josiah left school at the age of eleven and at first worked as a shepherd before going to sea as a cabin boy on the smacks Elizabeth and James and Mary, trading between the southern seaports of Wales and Ireland. In 1874, however, he was sacked for "breaking crockery" and decided to return to school. After two years at Towyn Grammar School, then under the direction of Mr Wallace James, he entered the Presbyterian College at Carmarthen and was ordained minister of Gwern-llwyn, Dowlais, in 1880. In 1885 he moved to New Bethel, Cwmaman and became a leading figure on the Liberal platform in close alliance with Thomas Edward Ellis of Bala and later with David Lloyd George. He believed fervently in Lloyd George's "Cymru Fydd" movement which both hoped would lead to Home Rule for Wales. In 1912 he won East Carmarthenshire for the Liberals and in 1917 he became Welsh Whip and Junior Lord of the Treasury. He always retained close links with New Quay where he had a home at 22 Marine Terrace and his daughters were educated at the Tutorial School. He died on 16th November 1925.

Ap Cei Newydd, who was a contemporary of Towyn Jones and recalled him as a small shy boy reciting a poem

The Rev Josiah Towyn Jones MP, Welsh Whip and Junior Lord of the Treasury. Courtesy of Mrs Ruth Wood.

at the New Quay Eisteddfod held at Black Lion Fields, wrote in the 1930s that "New Quay was always, and is now, overwhelmingly Liberal. Tories were few and far between. Well do I remember some of the Parliamentary elections of the old days and how partisan feelings ran strong. At one election all the singers who held the liberal creed were invited to Tabernacle to learn to sing certain doggerel to the tune of 'When Johnny Comes Marching Home'. Here is one verse:

Mi ganaf gan ar ding dong bell
Ding dong, ding dong,
I gladdu'r Tory er mor ddel
Ding dong, ding dong.
A hip hwre drwy wlad a thre
I Richard anwyl hyd y ne'
A ding dong bell ar fedd y Tory taer. (15)

To take part in this singing was regarded as almost a religious duty. Liberalism to many spelt liberty and freedom, while Toryism to some people stood for tyranny... On the night when the poll was declared there was great excitement and almost every house had lights in the window. There was one house, the house of a Mr Bateman in Church Street, a Conservative, with a lighted window decorated in red flowers the Conservative colour in Cardiganshire. It was remarkably pretty. Hundreds of radicals came to look at it and to admire it and no-one felt inclined to throw a stone through the window". As he concludes, this seems to prove that the standard of civilised behaviour in New Quay was high. (16)

The famous election of 1868 was recognised in Wales as a breakthrough into democratic politics away from the old "politics of deference", when the Tory squires had dominated Cardiganshire. The Second Reform Bill of 1867 had extended the franchise considerably. "The effect of which was to bring into the county constituency those sizeable seaports such as New Quay and inland townships such as Pontrhydfendigaid, where Nonconformity was strongly entrenched and well organised..." (17) No wonder there was such immense excitement in New Quay when Evan Matthew Richards of Swansea, a Nonconformist Liberal candidate was elected for Cardiganshire by 16 votes out of a total poll of 4,000. Great pressure was put upon tenants and a number were driven out of their homes when they refused to vote as their landlords required, though the figures of those dispossessed have been exaggerated in the past. The secret ballot, of course, was not introduced until 1872 and some tenants in the district were ejected from Plas Llanina land and built themselves the cottages at the "Arba", just outside New Quay. (19)

CHAPTER VI

The Royal Charter Storm, Lifeboats and the building of the Patent Slip

New Quay was at the height of its prosperity in the 1860s, despite suffering considerable damage during the Royal Charter Storm on 25th October 1859. This was one of the worst gales ever recorded, with winds of over 104 mph. It was named from the tragic loss of the great auxiliary steam clipper, the Royal Charter, wrecked at Moelfre, Anglesey with the loss of nearly all her 450 passengers and crew. Although 133 other vessels were lost in the same storm and 800 more lives, including the New Quay schooner Mathildis and her crew of six off the coast of Pembrokeshire, the magnitude of the Royal Charter tragedy caught people's imagination and the name stuck. Not only was it one of the greatest disasters of maritime history, but the Royal Charter was loaded with gold from the gold rush in Australia and many of her passengers were bringing home the fruits of their hard labour in the goldfields: they drowned because they would not abandon their heavy money-belts. (1)

The storm did a great deal of damage within the harbour at New Quay. The newspaper Baner ac Amserau Cymru reported from its "correspondent" that "the wind on Tuesday night was so strong no-one dared leave their homes. The harbour was quite full and the ships tore loose from their moorings and crashed into one another. On the morning of Wednesday when the wind had abated a little, the shore at New Quay was thronged with people come to see the extent of the damage and save what they might. The lighthouse and a big piece of the pier had gone. Below Fron-wig, the Pearl, recently repaired, was lying on its side against the rocks being battered by the waves; the Mary Hughes, the Perseverance and the Margaret & Anne were crashing together and being completely submerged at times by the huge seas. Behind Penpolion the Mary Eliza had sunk completely and the Ellen was on the rocks". According to oral tradition the Syren too was moored at Penpolion and during the storm her jib-boom lifted the roof off one of the houses on the beach, but as this incident is not recorded by our eyewitness, it must have occurred on another occasion. The Mary Anne, the smack Margaret and the Major Nanney were driven ashore at Traethgwyn; the Louisa Jane, another schooner and the smack Catherine were dragging their moorings and likely to drift with the rest. During the day, amazingly, the Mary Jane, Jane Morgans and the Robust, of Aberystwyth, and the Mary Jane of Chester, came in safely and in the evening the Gomer of Aberaeron. Although so much damage was done, only one person lost his life, one of the crew of the Major Nanney. But on the Thursday came the sad news of the loss of the Mathildis with Captain Joshua James, John Evans, his stepson and Owen Davies, Fron-wig aboard from New Quay. News was also received of damage to the schooner Eleanor of New Quay near Cardiff. However, three more survivors of the gale arrived safely, the schooner Equity on Thursday evening and the Susannah and Esther & Mary on Friday.

News came too of the loss of the Sylph, which was driven ashore near Conway: the crew and the captain's wife having to cling for hours to the rigging, the remainder of the vessel being under water and the sea so violent no-one could reach them, though in the afternoon coastguards succeeded in bringing them all safely to shore and they were taken by carriage to the Erskine Arms to recover from their terrible ordeal. Frequently even men died from exposure after hours in the rigging.

Three other ships were reported safe the same day: the Eliza, Mary and Heart of Oak; the Martha of Neath, which had sailed from New Quay on Monday evening with a local master, was reported on the rocks near St David's Head but the crew had escaped by climbing on to the rocks where they remained until dawn on Wednesday morning and were then seen and helped up to a nearby farmhouse.

Mr R W Jones and William Hopkin were sent for again to oversee the repairs to the pier which it was reckoned would cost between £1,000 and £2,000 and the tramway which had been allowed to fall into disrepair would have to be rebuilt. There was talk of extending the pier to provide the additional protection obviously required in such a gale, but nothing came of it. The damage was repaired and the familiar Pepperpot lighthouse took its place at the end of the quay to be a landmark for three-quarters of a century until swept away forever in another great storm in 1937.

The Royal Charter storm undoubtedly increased the pressure for a lifeboat to be established at New Quay. Since the wreck of the Venerable in 1818, there had been a number of other shipwrecks: the Hopewell, a 27 ton sloop, built at Craig Las and owned in New Quay from 1810, was wrecked there in 1829; in 1830, the sloop Jane of Aberystwyth struck New Quay Head and was totally lost. (2) She had been built at Aberporth in 1787 so had a long career at sea of over forty years. In 1832, the Royal George, 600 tons, bound for Liverpool, was

The Pepperpot Lighthouse, washed away after a storm in 1937.

only saved by cutting away her masts; and in the same year, the Nelly, master Captain Dick, stranded near New Quay. Ten years later, a heavy gale near New Quay caused the Aberystwyth sloop Anne & Betsey to be driven from her anchorage at New Quay and she became a total wreck. (3) A December gale of 1854 wrecked the New Jane with a coal cargo at New Quay, "a Christmas treat of free coal for the inhabitants". The following year, the Ivor (4), also carrying coal, experienced an explosion and fire severely damaged the ship, just off New Quay. The Board of Trade Wreck Chart reveals that out of 721 vessels lost off the British coast in 1861, 234 were lost between St David's Head and the Skerries and the Mull of Kintyre.

On 7th May 1864, Captain J B Ballard RN, Inspecting Commander of the Coastguard in the district, wrote to the Royal National Lifeboat Institution "on behalf of the residents of New Quay stating the need for a lifeboat, there having been thirteen wrecks in the area in the previous seven years with considerable loss of life". These must include some of the victims of the Royal Charter Storm and the Albert, 1858, the Lark, 1859 and the Danube, 1861, marked on Tom Bennett's maps of shipwrecks on this coast. (5) The RNLI agreed to the request and a Lifeboat House was built at the head of the pier. This was not a very convenient site for launching but the decision to build it there was probably taken because of the shelter provided by the harbour, but it meant that the lifeboat had to be hauled down on rollers, an extremely dangerous task, as demonstrated in the photograph, and then hauled back up by winch.

The first lifeboat based at New Quay was The Forester and she was formally presented in December 1864 and later renamed Nelson. This lifeboat was of course a pulling and sailing lifeboat as all New Quay's lifeboats were until 1949. What this meant in terms of manpower cannot easily be envisaged when one thinks of the crew struggling against the might of the gale as they had to on 16th October 1872 at dusk when, in heavy seas, they went to assist the Antigua of Greenock which had lost her main, mizzen and topmasts. In 1886 the Frank & Marian replaced the Nelson, named for her donors Frank and Marion Smart of Tunbridge Wells, who journeyed to New Quay for her launch. The Frank & Marion made several rescues over the years but the hazards of launching her down the pier became too great when one of the volunteers broke a leg. A new Lifeboat House was built at Penpolion and opened officially in 1904 by Mrs Longcroft of Plas Llanina. In 1907 the William Cantrell Ashley arrived at New Quay. She was to make history because she was to be the last pulling and sailing lifeboat in service with the Institution. The departure of the William Cantrell Ashley in 1949, the unique farewell to the last lifeboat of her kind in Britain, was recorded by the BBC. She subsequently had a varied career at the Outward Bound School in Aberdyfi and then in private ownership and for a while it was hoped she might become the nucleus of a Maritime Museum in New Quay but it was not to be. (6)

Although there were insufficient funds to extend the pier as suggested after the great gale of 1859, the Harbour Company was in a flourishing condition. By 1849 the tolls were bringing in £481/10/- a year and by 1851,

Launching the Frank & Marian.

according to the account books of E C L Fitzwilliams of Cilgwyn, (7) who was one of the largest shareholders, dividends of 10/- a share were being paid annually. Over a period of twenty years, he recouped his original investment and still had his shares as assets. In consequence, there was plenty of support for the decision to erect a Patent Slip at New Quay, to facilitate the considerable volume of ship repairs being undertaken there. Although fewer vessels were launched here in the 1850s than in the 1840s: 38 as opposed to 51, their average tonnage was higher and this decade too saw the launch of New Quay's most ambitious ventures so far: the barques Prince Llewelyn, Lettice Catherine and the Syren, in 1858 and 1859. This trend continued in the 1860s when 28 ships were launched with a total tonnage of 2870, compared to only 3343 for nearly twice as many ships in the 1840s. (8) This trend was also reflected in the tonnage of the vessels purchased from other ports, as will be seen below.

A Patent Slip is a large steel cradle which runs up and down an inclined permanent slipway on wheels and rails. At the lower end of the slipway the cradle is submerged, allowing the boat to be floated into the cradle and secured. A powerful windlass then hauls the cradle and boat up the incline clear of the water. Patent Slips can usually take the coasting type of vessel up to 500 tons and larger ones can handle boats of up to 1,000 tons.

Writing of the expansion of ship repairing and finishing at Appledore at this period, Basil Greenhill says: "A dry dock was wanted with proper industrial installations, a

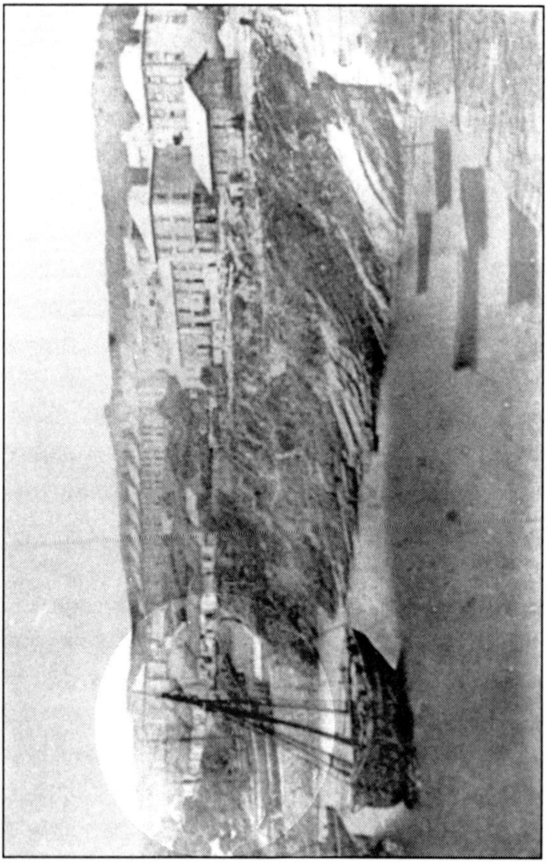

A schooner is on the Patent Slip in this rare early photograph of New Quay taken about 1870 on the left of the photograph, behind the stone wall running along the beach. Note the row of small cottages to the right above it. Around them newer houses have sprung up but Picton Terrace has not yet been built. The Lifeboat House can be seen on the right of the photograph. Author's collection.

foundry, a smithy, a sail-loft, block-making shops, a mast house around it, where ships could lie in complete safety with men working on them all day and all night if necessary.... Hence in 1855 the Yeos built a great dry dock at Appledore...The amenities provided.. made Appledore into the last seaport in Britain to be the base of a fleet of merchant sailing ships.. The great dry dock has kept Appledore ever since... It took two weeks to sheath a ship in metal in dry dock - on the beach it would have taken two months." (9) The dry dock at Appledore is now derelict but was active up to the 1980s. New Quay's Patent Slip and its accoutrements was an attempt to serve the same purpose.

In order to undertake the considerable expense of constructing the slip, the New Quay Patent Slip Company Ltd was formed under the Joint Stock Companies Acts of 1856/57 and fortunately its Day Book (10) has been preserved. This records the activities of the Company from 1863-1890. The Company was floated on 29th April 1862 on a capital of £2,000. The first entry was the payment of £145 to The New Quay Harbour Company for the site of the slip and a further £150 was paid to J B Attwood Esq for more land. John Attwood now owned most of Glyngoleu and farmed Coybal himself, his son was a solicitor in Aberystwyth and married to Mary Elizabeth Jones of Blaenau, a very old Merionethshire gentry family. (11) The steam engine to work the windlass was purchased from Mr Timothy Thomas, of the Foundry at Cardigan for £851/8/6$^1/_2$. The cost today would be at least £20,500. Captain Thomas Davies brought in a cargo of limestone for the company on the Eliza & Mary. Mary Jenkins, one of a number of women labourers employed in the 1860s and 1870s received 4/8½ for weighing the limestone. She must have been a strong woman. It is possible that she was a daughter of Anne Jenkins who lived at Penrhiwllan and was described in the 1851 Census as a "Nutt-mender", Mary would have been about 29 at this time.

Work continued throughout the summer and at times it appears from the immense list of names and payments detailed in the neat writing of Joshua James the Secretary, (who was also secretary of the Mutual Ship Insurance Society) that nearly every one in New Quay was employed on the work. Thomas Jones, painter, received two shillings for painting the name of the Company; labourers, masons, hauliers, carpenters, sawyers and smiths were constantly employed. Among the Directors of the Company were Evan Phillips, Master Mariner, who had shares in a number of New Quay ships and James Davies, shipbuilder, of Traethgwyn; the Auditors were James Jones, and Evan, son of the late David Timothy, who was a timber merchant. Evan Timothy & Co also managed the Ellen Catherine, the Emrys, the Kilvey and the Llaethlliw at various times (12). The Company's office was at the Glyn where they rented a room, Joshua Jones also lived there, and, as mentioned earlier, kept a school there in an upstairs room. John Davies was the Treasurer: this may well be John Davies, Albion House, a draper, who managed the Dreadnought, and was related to the Timothys by marriage. The Secretary received a salary of £4 a quarter, and the Treasurer, though apparently at first paid £5 a year, later received £5 a quarter.

In 1863 they had sold 140 shares at £10 each. Among the investors was Captain David Evans, Confidence, James Davies, Dolau Inn, John Jones, Sail-maker, Captain J Jones, Marwood, and Captain E Davies, Zenobia. The Company also had to borrow an additional £1446/19/0$^1/_2$.

The Patent Slip continued to employ a good many men and women when it was in operation, most being paid by the day and it seems to have generally been on a casual basis, as and when required. Labourers seem to have been paid about 2/- a day though three and a half days work earned James Jones 8/6. Daniel Davies "Old Dole" received 5/- for two and a half days' work. Hoblers, the men who helped unload the vessels are paid 1/- for "gathering blocks". In 1867 sawyers were paid 2/- a day and Thomas Evans "for sawing baulks" received 18/8$^1/_2$. David Evans was paid 5/- for "Cartage one tide": this would mean unloading a vessel while the tide permitted. Thomas Davies received 4/- "for getting the Car up". Very few ships' carpenters were identified as such apart from James Davies, who was on a retainer, and Jenkin Davies.

Evan Davies, Cei Bach, was one of the blacksmiths frequently employed: he was paid "the balance of his wages £5/10/-" on 6th March and £6/13/5 on 6th April, but then the next payment to him appears in September. One entry records that Jenkin Davies was paid for making mallets: these may have been caulking mallets to drive the oakum in between the planks of the ship to make it water-tight. In 1867 the masons Isaac and John Rees were paid £1/4/7 for work at the sawpit, which was

James Davies, shipbuilder, and his family at their home above Traethgwyn, an old building originally known as Storws Wen. James was the last foreman of the last active shipyard at New Quay. The house, later named Traethina, has unfortunately in 2011 begun to succumb to subsidence. Courtesy of Mrs David Highet.

probably constructed close to the cradle at the back of the beach. Owen Owens, blockmaker, was kept busy supplying wooden blocks for the rigging. In 1875 Joshua Jones, rigger, was paid 11/- but this is a rare entry. Labourers were employed in clearing mud - clay continues to surface today around the foot of the Lifeboat slip; "rising and relaying plates" and collecting and gathering wedges from the water. The car obviously suffered a good deal of wear and tear since it was always needing repair. It is nice to see that equal opportunity was alive and well in New Quay in the 1870s since the women labourers, Mary and Margaret Davies, seem to have received the same rate of pay as the men. Margaret John was paid 3/- for cartage in 1878. William and Timothy Thomas came up from the foundry in Cardigan to service the engine and were paid board and lodging as well. In 1877/78 a new boiler cost £65.

The Slip was kept busy and the same number of ships seem to have been handled in 1880 as in 1865-67 showing that New Quay continued to be fully engaged in shipbuilding and repairs. Between 1867-1870 nearly £500 was earned from 24 ships. Money was also earned from letting out the yard: handbills were posted at a cost of 5d to announce when it would be available. Thomas Davies was employed as a crier to go about the town to announce when assistance was required at the yard, or to summon people to a launching. This tradition of a town-crier persisted down until the 1950s, the last crier being Jack Lloyd, whose bell always attracted attention as he paused at a cross-roads and announced a dance or some other form of entertainment.

By 1861, just before the Patent Slip was erected, the number of shipwrights and ships' carpenters in Llanllwchaearn and Llanina had increased to thirty-three; though John Davies of New Quay alone described himself as a shipbuilder, along with Evan Daniel and Thomas James Thomas of Cei Bach. James Jones, Penlon Eglwys, was the only rigger actually named at that date. John Jones and John Edwards were still running their sail-rooms and had eight apprentices and journeymen between them. Wooden blocks for the rigging were being made by Owen Owens in Rock Street and by John Jones, Hafod, Llanina and John Jones employed an apprentice, Josiah Lewis. There were four sawyers at work in the sawpits on the beaches, and two rope-makers still active. A chandler's shop had been opened at 1 Glyn Square by Thomas Evans, next door to Jenkin Phillips, merchant. A foundry had been erected on the site of the present Council School and "Foundry Cottage" near Glanrhyd, was occupied by Morgan Jones from Cardigan, aged 28, who is described as an iron moulder. He produced pump handle windlasses and dolly winches for loading and unloading cargoes. The Patent Slip brought in increased work, and ten years later, in 1871, there were 38 ships' carpenters and shipwrights in New Quay, though four were not at home for the Census and may well have been employed at sea. John Davies, 4 Margaret Street, was building the Ina Lass, a 33 ton smack, later schooner-rigged, Evan Daniel was planning the brigantine Nymph at Cei Bach. (13) Altogether 40 vessels were acquired by the port in the 1860s, although only 13 were actually built there, the remainder being purchased from other ports.(14)

In 1871 there were nine sail makers, but only two sawyers at work and block-making was on the decline. Owen Owens still described himself as a blockmaker, but he was 82, and John Jones of Hafod had switched to carpentry and so had his son, David. The ropeyards and the foundry had closed down: Morgan Jones had left New Quay and his shop was occupied by Job John, blacksmith. By 1881 there were still 29 men employed as ships' carpenters, but a sign of the decline in shipbuilding and repairing meant that 15 of them were employed at sea, on big sailing ships; two, in their sixties, are listed as unemployed. Evan Daniel alone was still building ships at Cei Bach. Five sail-makers are mentioned, but two of them are the aged John Jones and John Edwards and they probably employed Thomas Davies, Rhiw-wig, William Langley of 1, South John Street and David Rees, George Street. Owen Owens had died at the age of ninety. John Jones, sail maker, though in his seventies, was running a chandlery business as well as his diminished sail-room. There were three sawyers at work and boys were still being apprenticed as ships' carpenters, for example David Davies, Cwm Noyadd, Llanina, to Evan Daniel.

Chapter VII

Ships and Sailors: The Coasting and Deep-water Trades

Shipbuilding and ancillary trades employed many, but the majority of New Quay's male inhabitants were sailors - 116 of them, at least, in 1851, and they came from neighbouring parishes too as it was a career which attracted many young men from the port's rural hinterland. In Chapter 1 I referred to the sailor-farmer, Owen Owen, Penparc, who retired from the sea in 1835 to farm. He died in 1852 but his sons, Thomas and John, went to sea and their widowed mother, Catherine, ran the 140 acre family farm. Thomas's father-in-law, David Evans, from the smallholding of Blaenllan, on the opposite side of the Cwm Tudu valley, also was at sea most of his life. Born in 1808, he was raised on the 18 acre smallholding; his father died young and David turned his hand to various jobs: labourer, mason, sailor, eventually remaining on the sea, while first his mother, then his wife, looked after the smallholding. Four of his five sons followed him to sea. The nearby Port of New Quay with its increasing fleet of ships offered them secure work, a better living and, above all, a hope of social advancement. David's youngest son, Captain Thomas Rees Evans (a first cousin of the famous Cranogwen, bard and teacher of navigation at Llangrannog) (1), was in a position, when he retired, to build himself a handsome house in the small hamlet of Pontgarreg, between Cwmtudu and Llangrannog and contributed £50 towards the building of a new chapel in Llangrannog. David's grandsons became ship owners in Cardiff. (2)

Owen Owen's younger son, John, first went to sea from New Quay when he was 14 years old, on the 58 ton schooner Mary Davies on 20th December 1853. She was newly launched by Thomas Davies of New Quay and the master was John's brother-in-law, Thomas Thomas Jones (sic) of Park Street, who had six shares in her. John's widowed mother also had a share in the Mary Davies. Most boys started out on this hard and dangerous life under the protection of relatives or neighbours. John Owen's career can be traced from his application to be examined for his Certificate of Competency as Only Mate (foreign-going trade) on 26th May 1860. From 1845 onwards, a system of examinations had been introduced for mates and masters. At first it was voluntary and applied only to foreign-going vessels, but it became compulsory from 1850, although exemption from the examinations was granted to those serving as masters and mates before that date, who could obtain Certificates of Service. However, unless carrying passengers, Certificates were not required, even after 1850, for the coasting trade and many masters in this trade at New Quay remained 'uncertificated' to the end of their days. John's older brother Thomas was one such, as master of the Union Packet, mentioned earlier. Where they have survived, these applications for Certificates are very useful to the family historian as they generally supply full details of the applicant's career at sea. The first step was usually to obtain a Second Mate's Certificate for which the candidate had to be 17 years' old and to have served four years at sea, although some, like John Owen, by-passed this qualification. The next step was an Only Mate's Certificate which had to be obtained before attempting the First Mate's qualification for which the age requirement was a minimum of 19 years. A candidate for a Master's Certificate had to be 21 years of age and have had six years at sea, of which one year had to be as First or Only Mate, and one year as Second Mate.

After three years on the Mary Davies as an Ordinary Seaman, John Owen spent some months ashore studying navigation and on 7th September 1857, he joined the brig Selina at New Quay. She was again a new ship, having been launched that year by John Anderton at Runcorn, Cheshire, registered as 199 tons. Her master was a fellow-Llandysuliogogo man, Thomas Jones. John Owen remained on the Selina until June 1858, voyaging to the Black Sea (3) and then returned to the Mary Davies as mate. (The Selina had a very short life as she was run down in the Sea of Marmora and lost on 20th March 1861). John took his Only Mate's examination at Cork on 26th May 1860. It was quite customary for local boys to take their examinations in Ireland and it was certainly more convenient than travelling to London. David Evans, Dol-wig, a near-contemporary of John's, obtained his master's certificate in Dublin and so did

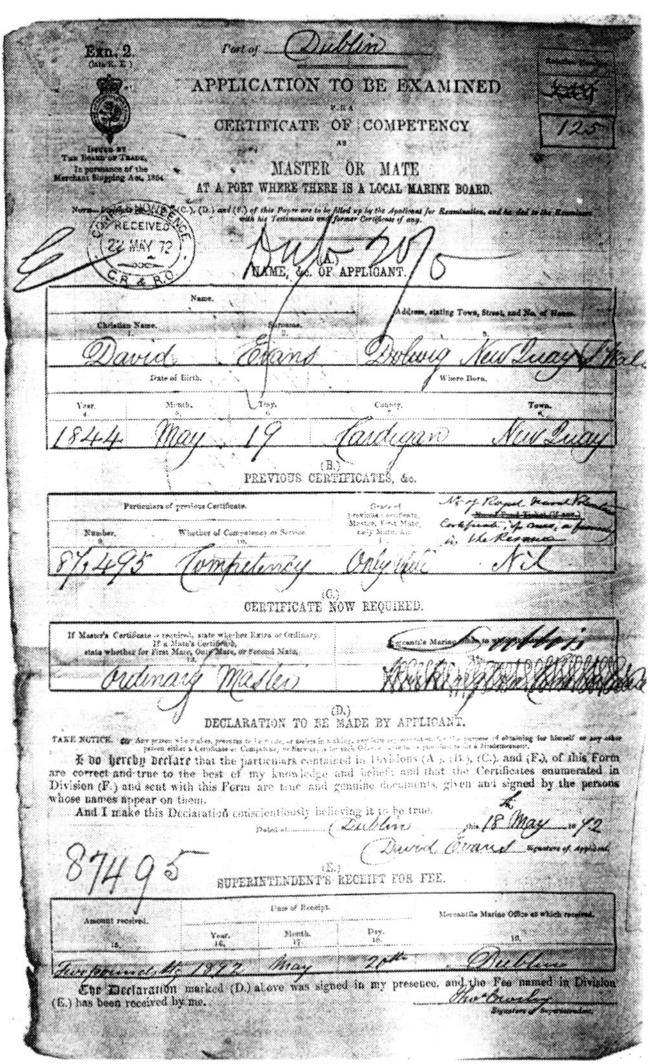

Exn. 2.

Issued by The Board of Trade, In pursuance of the Merchant Shipping Act, 1854.

Port of Dublin

APPLICATION TO BE EXAMINED

FOR A

CERTIFICATE OF COMPETENCY

AS

MASTER OR MATE

AT A PORT WHERE THERE IS A LOCAL MARINE BOARD.

125

RECEIVED 22 MAY 72 C.R. & R.O.

(A.)
NAME, &c. OF APPLICANT.

Christian Name. 1.	Surname. 2.	Address, stating Town, Street, and No. of House. 3.
David	Evans	Dolwig New Quay S Wal.

Year. 4.	Month. 5.	Day. 6.	County. 7.	Town. 8.
1844	May	19	Cardigan	New Quay

(B.)
PREVIOUS CERTIFICATES, &c.

Number.	Whether of Competency or Service. 10.	Grade of previous certificate, Master, First Mate, Only Mate, &c.	No. of Royal Naval Reserve Certificate, if any, as in the Reserve
87495	Competency	Only Mate	Nil

(C.)
CERTIFICATE NOW REQUIRED.

If Master's Certificate is required, state whether Extra or Ordinary. If a Mate's Certificate, state whether for First Mate, Only Mate, or Second Mate. 13.	Mercantile Marine Office to ... Dublin
Ordinary Master	

(D.)
DECLARATION TO BE MADE BY APPLICANT.

TAKE NOTICE. Any person who makes, procures to be made, or assists in making, any false representation for the purpose of obtaining for himself or any other person either a Certificate of Competency or Service, is for each Offence liable to be punished as for a Misdemeanour.

I do hereby declare that the particulars contained in Divisions (A.), (B.), (C.), and (F.), of this Form are correct and true to the best of my knowledge and belief; and that the Certificates enumerated in Division (F.) and sent with this Form are true and genuine documents, given and signed by the persons whose names appear on them.

And I make this Declaration conscientiously believing it to be true.

Dated at Dublin this 18th May 1872

David Evans Signature of Applicant

87495

(E.)
SUPERINTENDENT'S RECEIPT FOR FEE.

Amount received. 15.	Year. 16.	Month. 17.	Day. 18.	Mercantile Marine Office at which received. 19.
Two pounds	1872	May	20th	Dublin

The Declaration marked (D.) above was signed in my presence, and the Fee named in Division (E.) has been received by me.

Thos Bewley Signature of Superintendent.

David Evans, Dol-wig, New Quay: application for his Certificate as Ordinary Master at Dublin, 1872. Original at the National Maritime Museum.

John's uncle, Thomas Rees Evans, mentioned above, and all his brothers.

In 1860, John was first mate on the brigantine-rigged Elizabeth Jane of New Quay, built that year at Ipswich, Suffolk, by John Read. He made four voyages in her with Evan Evans, New Quay, as master. Then, like many local boys, John began to look further afield for his employment and his next berth was in the Borland of Liverpool as first mate from April until August 1862, to gain experience of bigger vessels, although the following year he was back on a New Quay ship as first mate of the brig Cambria, built at Cei Bach by Thomas James Thomas in 1853 and served on another local brig the Aeron Vale on voyages to the West Indies. In 1864, he obtained his Extra Master's ticket, the first man in Cardiganshire to do so. By 1869, he was in command of the Mackay, a barque of 384 tons, built at Miramichi, Prince Edward Island, and owned by Thomas & Co of Liverpool, sailing to the East Indies and thereafter he commanded the full-rigged ship W G Russell, built at Quebec and owned by J Thomas of Liverpool. Although the Liverpool companies often had their roots in the ports of North Wales and consequently employed many men from the Llyn peninsula and Anglesey, they employed a good many Cardiganshire mariners too. John Owen ended his days running a famous navigation school in Cardiff at Loudon Square, which was attended by many Cardiganshire mariners. Captain Picton Davies of Cardigan recalled in his old age that he had attended Captain Owen's school for his Second mate's square-rigged certificate in 1911: "while attending Captain Owen's school in the afternoon, the students were given problems to solve, based on the forenoon's lectures. This was the moment for Captain Owen to indulge in a little shut-eye". (He was, after all, over 70). "When well into his slumber, there was a quiet exodus from the class, a quick climb over the wall at the rear of the building into the nearest public-house, probably the old Cardigan Arms. After a quick drink the miscreants would return the way they came, to find their teacher sleeping peacefully. This recollection gave Captain Davies, himself then in his 80s, a great deal of pleasure." (4)

The transatlantic origins of John Owen's commands reflect a trend which was increasing, the purchase of wooden sailing vessels from Canada, generally from Prince Edward Island, often through the Island's agent, William Richards of Swansea. The story of this enterprising man and the even more interesting family into which he married, is told in Westcountrymen in Prince Edward's Isle. Because of the abundance of timber in the Canadian provinces, it was a good deal cheaper to purchase their vessels rather than build them in Britain from the imported timber, although in time British shipbuilders, by switching to iron and steel, responded to the challenge, but New Quay could not do so: it had not the resources.

Nevertheless, its investors did what they could and the 1860s and 1870s saw the purchase of a number of Canadian vessels, although only the smaller ones actually came to New Quay as the harbour could not accommodate the others. John Jones, the sail-maker, had shares in the Annie Ramsay, a 407 ton barque, built at Quebec and bought in 1863; the Derby, a 257 ton brig, built in Prince Edward Island and bought in 1867, the barquentine (5) Raymond acquired in 1876 - there is a photograph of her in Welsh Sail, and the Hero, a 362 ton barque acquired in 1879. Jenkin Phillips, Ifor House, bought the Pearl, a PEI brigantine built at New Bideford, in 1875 and, in the same year, with William Timothy, he purchased the 295 ton Adrienne, built at Vernon River, PEI, by Charles McDonald. (6) The writing was on the wall for sailing ships, however, and John Jones recognised this before his death in 1882: his son Jonathon had been apprenticed as a sail-maker in New Quay but in the 1870s he moved to Swansea and opened a successful ships' chandlers there.

Sailors too had to adapt to the changing times. John Owen's six nephews went to sea rather younger than he had, and certainly younger than the custom had been hitherto in New Quay, where, since the end of the 18th century, fourteen had been the usual age for a boy or apprentice. Even in the 1850s there were a number of fourteen year olds who had not yet joined ships. In the 1870s, one after another, the Owen boys joined ships at eleven years of age, although always "family" ships, the Mary Davies with their uncle Thomas Jones, and then the W G Russell with uncle John Owen, or the Jones Brothers with uncle Thomas Rees Evans. Then their pattern changed: although many New Quay men in command of larger vessels remained in sail till the end of their days, like Captain Edward Jones of the Adventurer of Liverpool; Captain David Davies of the Maxwell of Liverpool and the Glenogle; Captain Thomas Evans of the Harry of Swansea and the ill-fated Carnedd Llewelyn and Captain D O Thomas of the Illimani of Swansea, lost in the

The full-rigged ship Maxwell of Liverpool, commanded by Captain David Davies, who named his home in Park Street after his ship. Courtesy of the late Mrs John Rhydderch.

Columbia River in 1903, the younger generation switched to the new tramp steamers which were increasingly competing with the smaller sailing vessels in the carrying trades. The large sailing vessel grew larger in response to this competition - the vast four- five- and six-masted schooners and the "windjammers" of which Basil Lubbock has written with such zest (8) but these were too large for New Quay to handle as we have seen. However, her contacts with the sea were maintained, for generations she had bred mariners and they continued to go forth to serve in vessels from Glasgow to Newcastle-on-Tyne, though the most popular employers were the Cardiff-based shipping company Evan Thomas Radcliffe and Alfred Holt's Blue Funnel line of Liverpool and later still the great tankers of Shell.

Even in steam, the network of relationships which had operated so powerfully and effectively in sailing ship days continued. Men who had served their time "before the mast" were in great demand and a 'square-rigged ticket' still carried enormous cachet well into the twentieth century, my uncle Eddie Jones, a master for Shell, possessed one and so did my brother-in-law, John Rhydderch. Indeed, when Farmers & Figureheads was being written, only within a decade or so had we lost the last of the Cape Horners. The flow of mariners into the Merchant service continued until my generation. As the late Mr Sydney Fowler remarked to me, apropos of his own career at sea which began in the 1930s: "You never thought of doing anything else here". However, since those days, the United Kingdom's mercantile fleet is in decline and now only three New Quay men are at sea, including one in the Royal Navy.

As we have seen, New Quay's sailors began their careers in small local ships and earlier I referred to North Wales disbursement books which give valuable information about life at sea at the beginning of the 19th century. New Quay too possesses an interesting document relating to the coasting trade, for the middle of the 19th century, about the time John Owen began his career in the Mary Davies, though it could have been duplicated many times in the history of these little ships, which in other ports continued to work as late as 1960 but with auxiliary motors.

The Cargo Book of Theophilus Davies (9) of Dark Street, New Quay, master (and chief shareholder with 28 shares) of the smack Eliza & Mary, 43 tons, built in 1840 by David Davies, Ty'r Angel, covers the years 1848-1859 and is an unrivalled record of the coasting trade as it existed then. The book is written in his own inimitable way in a very Cymricised form of English. The following extracts are typical and the first is of particular interest since this took place in the "Hungry Forties" when Ireland was suffering from the great famine after the potato blight. The British Government was rather belatedly hiring as many vessels as it could to rush food to the desperate land where one million people died of starvation and related diseases.

Liverpool Disemper 27 1848

The a Count of a Cargo of Indian gorn we loaded to Waterford at 7/3 Ber tin

The frights amount sim of £22.9.6 (this is what he was paid for the voyage) -62 tin (tons)

(His expenses follow)

	£	s	d	
At Liverpool Comision on gargo	0	12	2	(for the agent)
Do Borters for stouin the gargo	0	8	6	(ditto Porters stowing)
Do gokin shor	0	7	6	(cooking ashore)
Do doakatmin	0	1	0	(docket man)
Waterford Bilats in apis (apiece)	0	2	6	(pilots' fees)
Do daklerasion for the gargo	0	1	0	(declaration)
The costman & harbor	4	11	0	(harbour dues)
Do for pone the Brights	0	2	0	(toll)
Do alauens	0	2	0	(allowance)
	6	19	8	

This left a profit of £15/9/0 but he would still have to pay the crew and it does not include food aboard either. It is unlikely there would have been more than three in the crew: the master, mate and a boy.

From Waterford he sailed to "Nuport", where, on 15th January 1849, he loaded a cargo of tin for Liverpool. In May he was at Lydstep in Pembrokeshire, where he loaded a cargo of limestone for New Quay:

The agount of a gargo of limston we loaded for Abram Thomas Llwnon (Llwynon farm, Llanina)

	£	s	d
Regived in Cash sim of	2	10	0
The fright amount sim of	14	17	6
Borters at listap & lawens (allowance)	1	5	0
Borters at New Quay	1	5	0
Hepe to the Bige	3	6	
(This must refer to getting the Eliza & Mary on to Cei Bach beach)			
	2	13	6
In cash with apram Thomas	2	10	0
In cash with mi wife	2	0	0
Do in cash	3	0	0

Abraham Thomas, it seems, chartered the Eliza & Mary with a part payment of £2/10/0 and paid the remainder at intervals. Later that same month Theophilus Davies was at Swansea, fulfilling another local charter:

The a Count of a gargo of golm (culm) we loaded to New Quay to John Enose (sic)

	£	s	d
The fright amount sim of	14	10	0
The expengis at New Quay Borters	1	0	0
Do Balast	0	7	6
Do harporduse on The vesl	0	10	8
Do Bilat in and out	0	3	0
	2	1	2

The Ballast would have been loaded at New Quay as the Eliza & Mary would have no cargo from there and then discharged at Swansea. Whether the pilot fees refer to Swansea or New Quay is unclear although one would imagine that Theophilus Davies would scarcely have needed their assistance at the latter, but perhaps harbour regulations specified that a pilot must be used. The three pilots operating at New Quay at this date were Benjamin Phillips, aged 52, who lived at the Dolau; James Davies, 55, who was from Llangrannog originally and lived at 3, Pengeulan and David Owens, 68, who lived at 13, Pengeulan. These were then the original small whitewashed cottages first built when New Quay became a maritime community. David Owens' son, also David Owens, lived in one of a pair of similar cottages known as America in Francis Street. He was the master of the Eleanor of New Quay, lost on a voyage from Limerick to Glasgow in February 1854 with his crew: John Evans, Dolau Uchaf, aged 44 and William Evans, Glyngolau, aged 21.

Theophilus Davies survived the many hazards of the sea. In a typical year he would visit Newport, Cardiff, Swansea, Llanelli, Ireland (Dublin, Waterford or Cork), Liverpool and Barrow in search of cargoes: carrying rails from Liverpool to Newport; wheat or "wet" as he wrote it, from Liverpool to "Gepstowe" (Chepstow); iron ore to Cardiff from Barrow, coal to Aberystwyth or Dublin from Swansea; occasionally he carried slates from Bangor to Waterford and oats from there to Newport; but most often he carried cargoes of limestone from Lydstep or Caldy to the little Cardiganshire ports, loading the limestone on the open beach below Lydstep's jagged cliffs in extremely dangerous conditions and then off-loading it between tides into carts provided by the farmers at Aberarth, Aberporth or Llangrannog. The

The women are mixing culm, the traditional home-made fuel of New Quay. Culm was fine coal (dust) imported regularly and mixed with clay and a little water to make briquettes. Although this must have been a very common sight, it has attracted two children from their play and even older ones have stopped to watch the experienced workers. Note the excellent condition of the cottage in the background: the snug thatch, the sturdy freshly white-washed walls, the comparatively large opened windows, a far cry from the dilapidated ones with their apparently hermetically-sealed windows so often illustrated as the hovels of the poor. But almost every cottage in New Quay was as snug and attractive as this one.

furthest he ever sailed was a voyage from Liverpool to Rouen, the only time he crossed the Channel in the Eliza & Mary and this was still classed as Home Trade. It was his most profitable trip earning £52/2/6d. By 1865 he was the master and sole owner of the 125 ton schooner, Ellen Catherine, built by Owen Owens at Traethgwyn in 1850; when he felt too old to continue going to sea, he put in a master and became a pilot at New Quay.

He was both skilful and lucky and so were many others but there were many problems apart from lack of cargoes and tricky landing places. The sailing ship was utterly dependent on the wind and it was this dependence and the consequent uncertainty of her voyages which eventually led to her displacement by the tramp steamer. The 1867 Log of the Active, a 97 ton schooner owned by John Evans, Morfa Gwyn, and whose master was his son Francis, aged 19, demonstrates some of the problems which bedevilled the sailing ship:

September 11	Sailed from New Quay to Bristol Channel in Ballast Wind SSE
September 14	Arrived Mumbles Wind NNW
September 17	Sailed from Swansea with a cargo of culm for Mr Macarmie, Kingston, (Ireland)
September 25	Arrived at Kingston Wind WNW strong
October 12	Sailed from Kingston Wind WNW light
October 15	Put back into Kingston windbound, Wind S by E strong
October 19	Sailed from Kingston Wind NNW light
October 21	Arrived at the Mumbles Wind SSW strong and rainy

October 22	Sailed into the New Cut Swansea
October 23	Towed to the South Dock where cargo discharged.
November 2	Towed out of South Dock by Steam Tug Rescue bound for Belfast with a cargo of culm for Mr MacColag Wind E calm
November 8	4 pm Towed up to Belfast by Steam Tug Vesta Wind WNW moderate
November 24	9 am Sailed from Belfast in ballast for Whitehaven Wind W strong
November 25	10 am Arrived in Whitehaven Wind strong W
November 27	3 pm Commence to discharge ballast
November 28	4 pm Got all our ballast out 45 tons
November 30	8 am Commence to load pig iron for Newport
December 2	11 pm finished loading pig iron
December 3	4 pm sailed from Whitehaven Wind S bound for Newport
December 5	3 pm Split our topsail. Put back for Beaumaris. Windbound Wind W strong.
December 22	5 am Sailed from Beaumaris Wind moderate W
December 23	11 am Put into Holyhead owing to it blowing too hard from the WSW to beat down the Channel.
December 25	8 am Sailed from Holyhead Wind NW Wind came to WSW
December 29	8 pm Put back from Caldy Island to Milford Haven. Windbound Wind ESE Foggy
December 30	6 am Came to anchor in Hakin

December 31	9 am Sailed from Milford Haven Wind ENE strong 6 pm Wear ship again for Milford 10pm Came into Angle Wind ESE strong
1868	
January 3	Sailed from Milford bound for Newport Wind ENE
January 4	Arrived Newport 1 pm Wind NE strong
January 6	Towed up to berth. (10)

It had taken more than a month to complete the voyage from Whitehaven to Newport and Basil Greenhill in The Merchant Schooners relates that some ships were wind bound for six weeks or more.

Both the Eliza & Mary and the Active were typical examples of the coasting trade, but others sailed the seven seas. A record of the voyages of the Sarah Bridget has survived for the years 1866-1868 (11), which throws some light on the Foreign Trade. She was one of the vessels purchased from other ports by New Quay ship owners, perhaps because of their builders' good reputations or because they were available at a time when their purchasers were looking for a good investment: some were certainly commissioned like the Elizabeth Jane from Ipswich, mentioned earlier. The Sarah Bridget was a 126 ton brigantine, built by Edward Ellis at Bangor in 1858. In 1866 her master was Joshua Griffiths, Certificate Number 1154. In March 1855 she sailed from Cardiff for Genoa, probably with a cargo of coal although this isn't specified in her Crew Agreement or Log and on to Gallipoli before returning to Glasgow

Francis Evans, son of John Evans, Morfa Gwyn, in his old age at the Arba, New Quay with his wife Sarah and his sons, from left to right, Daniel Owen (who was New Quay's last surviving Cape Horner), Thomas James, Josiah Raymond, who was lost at sea in WWI, and David Luther in army uniform. Also in the photograph is their daughter Sarah. Courtesy of Mrs Melita Evans.

to discharge; in 1867 she went from Antwerp to Athens and Smyrna and in 1868 from Dublin to Cette, Patras and Prevesa, Greece. The average crew she carried was about seven in number and they were a mixed bunch, sometimes local and sometimes men recruited at foreign ports. In 1868 the Captain was aged 37; the mate was Thomas Jones, 25, of New Quay, Certificate Number 86022, whose previous ship was the Hope of Newport. The Able Seamen were John Jacobs, 19, of Antwerp, making his second voyage in the Sarah Bridget: on the first he had been an Ordinary Seaman and Cook and Steward, which earned him 5s a month on top of his £2 OS pay; as an AB he earned £2/10/- a month; the second was Jenkin Jones, 55, of New Quay, whose previous ship was the Jane & Mary of New Quay; and John Lusignan, aged 32, from Argyle, formerly on the Rose Alice of Liverpool. The two Ordinary seamen on this voyage were Cornelius Le Brun, whose previous ship was the Mercator of Rotterdam and Franz de Erilles of Antwerp who had previously served in the Sarah Bridget as a boy, for which he had received £1 a month. The mate received £4/10/-. As is usual the Captain's pay is not given. This was often negotiated with the owners.

The Newfoundland trade provided another important source of New Quay's income. The Friendship, the Hind, the U'Larsing, the Ceredig and the Dreadnought are all known to have been employed in this trade and so were the Prince Edward Island-built ships like the Resolven and the Pearl. The tremendous quantities of cod found in the shallow seas off Newfoundland and Nova Scotia and in the Gulf of St Lawrence attracted European fishermen from the end of the 15th century. Salt fish was an important item in European diet, easily preserved in a technically primitive society before the days of canning and freezing food. By its nature this was a small ship trade for the small harbours and quays of Newfoundland and Labrador could not accommodate large vessels. The great Newfoundland merchants: Munn & Company of Harbour Grace, and C T Bowring of St John's and Liverpool, instructed brokers in Bristol and Liverpool, who chartered small schooners from Wales and the West Country for the European trade. A typical voyage would be coal to Cadiz from Swansea, salt to Newfoundland and back to the Mediterranean with salted cod. It was an exacting trade and generally only one or two passages were made each season. Nearly every home in New Quay once had paintings of Vesuvius in eruption and some had paintings of their vessels entering Naples Harbour. Enterprising Italian painters had the backgrounds already prepared and the vessel could be added quickly while the master was in harbour. Not quite painting by

The Brig Alert entering Naples Harbour. Courtesy of Dr Valerie Bowen.

numbers but certainly on the conveyer belt principle. Even so the results are most attractive.

The pattern of Newfoundland trade is confirmed by a letter which survives from 1880, addressed to Captain William Phillips, Schooner Hind, Post Office, Newfoundland, and full of fascinating gossip with a maritime flavour. It is from his daughter Elizabeth, who lived at 3, Lewis Terrace, New Quay. She writes: "I have sent you a letter this long time to Cadiz... Anne Lloyd Hedessa is married last week to a young man from Cardigan, Captain of a very large barque and she is going with him for three years of voyage but nobody thinks she will live to come back to England also I think I have told you in the other letter that Mary Ellen Jones Hagar (12) is married to the minister of Capel Wig and I think that there is nobody in the world so happy as them, also William Phillips Wellington is home now he was in the Sea Queen and the vessel went on fire when on their way home to England all the crew were saved but all of them lost their clothes.."

The Hind was a two-masted 115 ton schooner with a young deer figurehead, built at Cardiff in 1862 and transferred from Liverpool to New Quay in 1879 when she was purchased by John Owen, farmer, of Ciliau, Llandysuliogogo and William Phillips with 32 shares each. William Phillips had to borrow to purchase his half of the vessel and mortgaged his shares for £310 but by 1885 had earned enough money to discharge the mortgage. The hapless Anne Lloyd, for whom the gloomy forecast was made, was the daughter of Griffith Lloyd, master of the Hedessa, who died in 1873 aged 66. The Hedessa was a schooner of 92 tons, launched at

Traethgwyn by John Davies in 1853. She was sunk after a collision in the English Channel in 1891. The Hagar, 122 tons, was also a schooner, built at Chester in 1858 and lost off Ushant in 1879, a year before the letter was written. The Hind was sold to Padstow in 1891. The Sea Queen was a schooner, built at Bideford in 1858 and owned in Aberystwyth.

As we can see, Captains and their families were invariably referred to by the soubriquet of their ships and this practice continued for many years after those vessels had been sunk, sold away or broken up. The Susannah Knapp, a brig of 178 tons, built at Port Hill, Prince Edward Island, by James Yeo and owned in New Quay from 1863, was lost off the French coast in 1883, but her master's daughter was known as "Miss Davies, Susannah Knapp" for over sixty years after that date. Houses were often named after favourite ships and these names are an integral part of New Quay now and conjure up for passers-by the vanished ships like Confidence, Loyalty, Zenobia, Pearl, Kilmorie, Lynwood and Almora and many more, although unfortunately some house names have been altered in recent years, like Utopia in Park Street and U'Larsing in Hill Street.

The brig Utopia was built by Hoad Brothers, Rye, Sussex in 1860 with a registered tonnage of 184. She was transferred to New Quay ownership in 1867. The master was David Davies, eldest son of the late Moses Davies, weaver, of Mason Street "on Perthygwenyn land", New Quay where he had been born in 1836. His father had died when David was very young and his mother Dinah married another weaver and continued to occupy the

These unique sketches of local ladies were made by Mrs Myra Evans, whose delightful recollections of New Quay in the 1890s and early 1900s, published as Atgofion Ceinewydd, are still in print. Retriever, Lynwood, Zenobia, Susannah Knap (sic) and Osaka are all names of ships. Author's Collection.

same house. Weavers might earn as little as 8s a week and it was natural that Dinah should send her sons to sea where the opportunities to better their lot were far greater. David obtained his Master's Certificate in Dublin in 1862. When he took command of the Utopia in 1867, his younger brother Lewis became the mate and there were four other New Quay men in the crew and one from Cardigan, while the cook came from Memel, Lithuania. The pattern of her voyages between 1867 and 1882 demonstrates how far New Quay's comparatively small brigs ventured on regular voyages.

1867 Mediterranean, South America
1868 West Coast of Africa
1869 West Indies
1870 United States: she was dis-masted in a gale this year
1871 West Indies and the Mediterranean
1872 West Africa
1873 West Indies
1874 West Indies
1875 West Indies and West Africa
1876 Australia
1877 West Indies
1878 South Africa
1879 no record
1880 South Africa
1881 West Indies and West Africa
1882 United States (14)

This was David Davies' last voyage for he died in Brooklyn, New York and was buried there. He was only 47 years old. Of his four sons, three died in childhood, two within a few days of each other in October 1874, aged five and two, probably of scarlet fever which carried off a number of children that year. Owen Davies, the blacksmith, lost two small daughters in November 1874 to that disease. Another of David's sons died at the age of two in 1877 and the only survivor, John Moses, drowned on a voyage from Barry to Buenos Aires in November 1905 aged 32. Such a tragic history was not at all exceptional.

After twenty years at sea, as master of several New Quay ships, including the brigs Aeron Vale and Cambria, his brother Lewis retired from the sea and became a farmer at Cefn Bach, Brynhoffnant, Cardiganshire, where he died in 1887, being described as farmer on his gravestone, with no reference to his long career at sea. This is unusual, but otherwise his change of career, as we have seen, was not untypical of local mariners, many of whom came from the land and returned to it when they retired from the sea or acquired property with the money they earned and set themselves up for the first time in the history of their families as landowners. His younger brother John was lost on the Anne Leslie of Swansea, which sailed from Saffi, Morocco, with a cargo of grain, in November 1886, and was never heard of again.

The house, once proudly named Osaka, in Church Street, has long changed its name but local people still recalled the original name and the career of the vessel from which it derived. The Osaka belonged to the noblest class of ships: the tea-clipper. Basil Lubbock, the doyen of writers about sailing ships, was a man who knew and loved these heroines of the greatest days of sail and has commemorated many of them in The China Clippers. This book is dedicated to:

"The sailor of the Sail...
Lord of the bunt, the gasket and master of the yard
To whom no land was distant, to whom no sea was barred".

All sailing vessels have a grace denied the more practical steamship which eventually replaced them but none perhaps have captured the imagination of the general public as much as the China tea-clippers with great names like Ariel, Thermopylae, Taeping and Cutty Sark, the last-named luckily preserved through the efforts of Captain Dowman of Trevissome, Devon. A painting of the Cutty Sark hung in our sitting-room and my father never tired of telling me as I never tired of hearing the stories he himself had heard as a child of the amazing feats of these great ships.

The China tea trade was originally in the hands of the East India Company until its monopoly ended in 1834 but even thereafter the tea trade remained on a small scale until well into the 1840s when the opening up of more treaty ports in China led to an increase in the export of tea. The Americans were the first to build tea-clippers and the amazing passage of the Oriental from Hong Kong to the West India Docks in London in 97 days in 1850 soon led to British emulation. The tea trade races lasted for about twenty years and every year the races were eagerly followed through the newspapers. The crews took immense pride in their vessels and would even wager a month's wages on the outcome. The Osaka was one of the last of the speedy vessels launched for this trade: built for a man who made his name as master of the Challenger, one of the fastest vessels of all time with passages of 105 days from Shanghai. Captain Killick founded the firm of Killick and Martin and eventually owned the well-known clippers, Kaisow, Omba, Wylo, Osaka and Lothair. The Osaka was a small clipper barque built by Pile of Sunderland in 1869. There is no record of her performance in The China Clippers but the Kaisow raced home once from Foochow in 99 days, beating the Thermopylae and the Taeping. An American nicknamed Lothair "The Flying Dutchman" since she overtook his ship making 17 knots.

"The year 1872 may be said to be the last year in which there were any real races among the clippers. Henceforward, although the captains still did their best to make fast passages, they no longer had the chance of bringing the first teas to market, because they were taken by racing steamers through the Suez Canal." (15) Nevertheless on other passages there continued to be the cachet of being in command of some of the fastest and most beautifully designed vessels ever launched. No wonder that Captain Jones was proud to name his home after his finest command.

Not only houses but children too had exotic names to commemorate their fathers' voyages, Christian names being selected because the child was born at sea or because the father was in a particular port at the time. Among the more unusual names borne by New Quay children were Brisbane, Chile and Valdivia, after the port on the West coast of South America. Everyone who went "deep sea" had rounded the Horn at one time or another and it was not an experience only for hardened sailors but one known to schoolgirl daughters, like Agnes, daughter of Captain Thomas Evans, Park Street, who commanded the full-rigged ship, Carnedd Llewellyn. It seems appropriate to end this brief survey of the typical voyages of New Quay vessels with the most testing of them all, the South American run, in a study of the experiences of the New Quay barque Syren, launched in 1859 by Thomas James Thomas, Cei Bach and owned by Evan Thomas & Co, Cambrian House, New Quay. Her first master was Captain Griffith Jones, a son of Oernant Farm, Llanina, who married Martha Evans, Neuadd and lived at Prospect House, New Quay. He was drowned off Portugal in 1870 and the mate brought the Syren home.

"Agreements and Accounts of Crews" relating to the Syren (16) survive for the 1880s and give an interesting picture of the workings of a typical small barque in the last days of the smaller sailing vessels in Foreign Trade. At 296 tons the Syren was only a quarter or even an eighth of the size of the last of the windjammers which soon became the only sailing ships capable of persevering in the face of declining freights. Captain Edward Jones, who took command of the Syren in February 1881, exemplified in his career too the opportunities to be seized in New Quay by those from impoverished backgrounds. He was born in 1842, the youngest son and eighth child of a weaver in Cwmtudu and three of his siblings died in infancy. He went to sea at the age of nine and served on local vessels. At the age of twenty he was an AB on the Milford barque Economist trading to the Mediterranean. He was subsequently mate on the 130 ton Hawendale, built at Traethgwyn in 1858 and on the schooner Active of New Quay; he also served on the Renown of Swansea, another coasting schooner. His first command was a similar vessel: the Margaret of Cardigan in 1870.

Alan Villiers, in a chapter headed "Masters Most Vulnerable", among his strictures on incapable masters in The War with Cape Horn, pays tribute to men like Captain Edward Jones, who had learned their trade thoroughly: "who began young and stayed long" in small ships. "A boy in Scots, Welsh or Devon short-voyage schooners, brigantines and the like learned cargo stowage... and got plenty of experience. The trim - the seat in the water - of sailing ships was a very important point in both their sailing and earning. A properly-trimmed ship loaded more, strained her rigging less and sailed better... Seamen learned these things better if they served in smaller ships first". (17)

In 1878, Edward Jones joined the Feodore, managed by Evan Phillips, formerly of Marine Terrace, New Quay and now a ship-broker in Swansea. Although Swansea's great days as a copper-ore port were nearly over, her docks were still expanding to cope with exports of coal, patent fuel and anthracite. Here Evan Phillips was well placed not only to arrange freights but also to purchase Prince Edward Island-built vessels for New Quay owners, through their Swansea agents, William and Thomas Richards. The Feodore, a salted (18) brigantine of 187 tons, had been built by John Lefurgey in 1877, who also built the Raymond, referred to earlier. Appropriately she was in the Newfoundland trade: carrying cargoes of coal from Swansea to Cadiz, salt to the

Canadian provinces and taking fish back to Europe. In 1880 Edward Jones finally obtained his Master's Certificate at Swansea. He had had very little early education which probably accounted for his tardiness in doing so, for he was then 37; he had not required it earlier since he was not carrying passengers, but although he had commanded the Feodore successfully on earlier voyages, the owners obviously felt, possibly for insurance requirements, that he should be certificated. Unfortunately, while on a voyage from Madeira to Malpeque, PEI, the Feodore went ashore in a severe gale at Savage Harbour, PEI, that November and became a total loss. (19) Her crew were saved and Edward Jones returned home to take command of the Syren.

Her previous master was Thomas Thomas of New Quay, born in 1846. He had just brought her into Milford after a voyage from Cardiff to Fray Bentos on the River Plate, South America, and she was there two months before Edward took her over. This long stay at Milford between voyages, which occurred at least twice in the 1880s, is an indication that New Quay no longer offered the kind of services required to refit larger vessels. In 1867 the Syren had been overhauled here on the Patent Slip. But this was the only entry for her in the account book. Edward took the Syren around to Cardiff in a day, with the aid of a temporary crew of New Quay sailors, who included his son John Edward Jones, aged 14, having his first taste of the sea. The mate was Thomas Jones of New Quay aged 29, whose previous ship was the Ivanhoe of Aberystwyth, and the second mate was Evan Evans, 22, also from New Quay, who had previously been on the schooner Ellen Ann. The Syren had accommodation for ten crewmen but eight was her normal complement, plus one apprentice. At Cardiff she loaded coal for Cape Town and sailed on May 15th, but a collision in crowded Penarth Roads with the Norwegian barque Frank led to her having to be towed back to port for repairs. She sailed again on 8th June and reached Cape Town on August 30th. John Thomas, one of the ABs who gave his place of birth as James Town and his previous vessel as the Unomis of Scarborough and was, unusually for that period, illiterate, had to be left there in hospital and his wages of £2/3/1 (he had already been advanced £2/10/- when he joined the ship) were given to the Assistant Shipping Master there to keep for him. No indication is given of what ailed John Thomas. The wages for the crew at this time were: Mate: £5/10/- a month; Second Mate: £3; the "Cook & Seaman" who was David Jones of New Quay, received £3/10/-; Able Seamen: £2/10/-; and Ordinary Seamen, depending on age and experience, from £1/15/- to £2/5/-. It will be observed that Able and Ordinary Seamen were not much better off than they had been at the turn of the century. Masters earned about £10 a month though they could also count on 'perks', such as carrying goods to trade on their own account. In addition, the 'Slop Chest' was the Master's responsibility, offering an opportunity to make some profit. From the Slop Chest the crew was kitted out if they had insufficient gear of their own, the cost being deducted from their wages.

A Slop Chest list from the barque Doune Castle has survived, (20) listing the items purchased by her master, Captain Thomas Jones, Adpar, New Quay, from The Golden Goat, Jones & Co, 226 High Street, Swansea, on

4th February 1891, before he went to join the Doune Castle at Middlesbrough on Tees.

	£	s	d
8 Blutcher (sic) Boots @ 5/6	2	4	-
6 pair Slipper @ 2/11 1/2.	-	17	9
4 Pair Short Sea Boots @ 13/-	2	12	0
4 pair High Sea Boots @ 16/11	3	7	8
4 Best sewn canvas shoes @ 5/9	1	3	0
12 Flannel Drawers @ 1/11	1	3	0
18 Best dungaree trousers@ 1/11	1	14	6
12 Dungaree Jackets @ 2/-	1	4	0
12 Alma Caps @ 9 1/2.d	-	9	6
12 Best Alma Caps @ 10 1/2.d	-	10	6
6 Caps with lugs (ear-flaps) @ 1s 2d	-	7	0
12 Holland Hats @ 7 1/2d	-	7	6
3 Cardigan Jackets @ 4/11	-	14	9
3 Best Cardigan Jackets in boxes @ 10/6	1	11	6
24 Pair Stockings @ 1/-	1	4	0
12 Merino singlets @ 1/9 1/2.	1	1	6
6 Merino drawers @ 1/11	-	11	6
12 Pair Merino sox @ 6d	-	6	0
6 All double oil suits @ 8/6	2	11	0
6 Cloth trousers @ 4/11 1/2.	1	9	6
12 Crimean Shirts @ 1/11	1	3	0
12 All wool shirts @ 2/11	1	15	0
12 Fine Ceylon shirts with collars @ 3/-	1	16	0
12 All wool shirts @ 3/11	2	7	0

6 Towels @ 3½d	-	1	9
1 Tweed Suit @ 21/-	1	1	0
1 Dark Plaid Suit @ 25/6	1	5	6
1 Best Scotch Tweed Suit @ 27/6	1	7	6
1 Serge Suit @ 20/1	1	0	1
12 Jac Knifes (sic) @ 8½d	-	8	6
12 sheath Knifes (sic) @ 5½d	-	5	6
12 Wide belts @ 6d	-	6	0
12 Sheaths @ 3d	-	1	6
6 Mufflers @ 1/-	-	6	0
12 Pairs mittings (sic) @ 9½d	-	9	6
2 Pair Brown Blankets @ 4/3	-	8	6
Insurance	1	7	6
	£40	19	11
1 Box Soap not charged	1	12	4
	£42	2	5

Perusing the list one can conclude that it would not be the Captain's fault if the men were not properly kitted out, and certainly he purchased some good quality clothes, Merino is the superior Australian sheep's wool. It is interesting to note echoes of great wars of the past in some of the items: Blucher of course was the famous Waterloo general; and Alma and Crimea recall the war of the 1850s with Russia. One cannot help speculating that the Ceylon shirts were included for the Captain's private trading and perhaps the suits too.

To return to the Syren: she left Cape Town on 20th September in ballast, for Ichabo island on the coast of West Africa to load guano, which she discharged at Leith, arriving there on 13th January 1882. In nearly three years, from 1881 to 1884, Edward Jones would only have five weeks altogether in British ports. He had three of those weeks at Leith and was outward bound again for Demerara, British Guyana, on 6th February 1882. The crew of course were free to go home if they wished and this time his mate was John Thomas of New Quay, aged 69, who must have been one of the oldest men serving deep sea at this time; his previous ship had been the Elizabeth Jane, owned by Jenkin Phillips, Glyn, New Quay. David Jones, New Quay, continued aboard as the Cook. Three of the ABs were Scandinavians, one from Denmark and two from Finland, who had been serving together on the Olive Branch of Peterhead, Scotland. Edward Jones frequently carried Scandinavian and German crews picked up in Hamburg: among them Henry Christian Moller, who accompanied the Captain to New Quay after one voyage and liked it so well he settled there and established a family which flourishes there to this day, still retaining their Scandinavian fairness but otherwise entirely Welsh. The combination of poor terrain and a long seaboard, as in Wales, brought as many Scandinavians to sea as Welshmen and they were deeply involved in the last days of sail.

The cargo of sugar collected at Demerara was discharged at Hamburg in August 1882. Here the Captain had an opportunity to see his family again, for his wife Eliza, (daughter of John Thomas, the New Quay pilot) travelled out to meet him with their son and John joined his father's

On the left of this group is Henry Christian Moller from Christiania (Oslo), with his wife, a local girl, and their family. Courtesy of the late Mr Aneurin Moller.

ship as an Ordinary Seaman; still on board from the previous voyage was another young Welshman, Richard Jones from "Beauford", Brecon, but the remainder of the crew were German and Scandinavian including the mate Hans Kohler. On 29th September the Syren was outward bound for Pernambuco accomplishing the passage in forty-nine days. After discharging her cargo at Hamburg again, she sailed to Cardiff to collect a cargo of coal and in May 1883 was outward bound to Fray Bentos. The mate was William Jones of Aberaeron and among the crew were three Portmadoc men. John Evans, an apprentice, was also still on board, along with the Captain's son.

They picked up the 'nortada' off the Portugese coast and then the trade winds that would send the Syren scudding smoothly along till the doldrums "with their nervous cat's paws of fleeting airs, their sudden swift squalls, their deluge after deluge of almost solid rain". (21) But these were always welcome on board ship where fresh water supplies were always limited and the crew would take impromptu showers on deck "clad only in a cake of soap" (22). As Captain Piening, one of the most famous of Cape Horn sailors described it: "Sailing through this region makes special demands on the shipmaster. To a high degree, it depends on his knowledge and experience how long the passage will be delayed here. The belt of calms (doldrums) lies diagonally across the Atlantic like a wedge with its broad end on the African coast, narrowing towards the west. Once through the wedge, he will find the south-east trade wind; but there are currents in this doldrums zone too, and they can set me towards Brazil... If I foolishly allow the ship to get too far to the west... I can find the bulge of Brazil getting in my way and have to work back before sailing south again... In the area of the great La Plata River - the River Plate - we keep wary watch for the first sign of those overheated violent bursts of pampas winds sailors call pamperos... We watch for the telltale sausage-like cloud bank which, briefly seen, turns rapidly into the dangerous pampero. Just note the ends of that sausage cloud begin to droop like a Chinese mustache: then stand by the halyards... getting the best out of your ship does not include foolish chances. For the pampero comes with a mad haste that frightens the sea itself so it lies flat, as if all the wind on earth had struck it at once, like a an enormous roller flung along at 100 knots". (23)

The Syren reached Fray Bentos safely, collected a return cargo of guano from Independencia and sailed for Liverpool in September 1883 arriving there after a voyage of ninety-nine days in the New Year of 1884. She continued to sail from Cardiff or Leith for South America until 1887, by which time she was 28 years old. Perhaps the ship was showing signs of wear. The previous Crew Agreements show that in these six years only one crew member had jumped ship in South America, a good record, but when the Syren reached Buenos Aires on 21st July 1887 her three Scandinavian ABs deserted, possibly they had a premonition of disaster. Of the remaining crew, the mate was Henry Harries of Aberaeron, aged 25, and John Smith of Georgia, was the Cook and Seaman; the Ordinary Seamen on this voyage were Johan Jensen, a Norwegian, David Jenkin Jones of New Quay, aged 16, whose previous ship had been the Swordfish of Swansea, and J M Logan of Newhaven, whose first ship this was. Three more crewmen were found to replace the deserters, including William Elliott from Leith, aged 22, who had never served at sea. This suggests that William had emigrated to South America to work, and now homesick, he could not afford the return journey other than by volunteering as a seaman. As a 'boy' he was paid 10/- a month. Henry Evans, aged 58 from Caernarfon, who had previously been aboard the Oronsa, and Thomas McKewen aged 45 from Baltimore were the other replacements. All three may have been supplied by the notorious crimps who operated in all the major ports, even kidnapping men from their lawful ships, getting them drunk and then "selling" them for thirty dollars apiece to desperate shipmasters.

According to the Crew Agreement, the Captain collected her Articles, which had to be deposited at the Consul's office on arrival at a port, on 16th August 1887. Thirty-nine days out she foundered at sea. Possibly the Syren had strained her planking in heavy weather and was shipping more water than the pumps could cope with. Fortunately for her crew, having taken to the boat, they were picked up by the French barque Indien of Marseilles and in December found themselves back in Buenos Aires once more. Four years earlier, the same fate had overtaken her sister ship, the barque Prince Llewelyn, off St Thomas, West Indies. The only other New Quay-built barque, the Lettice Catherine, had been lost at Bahia Blanca nearly twenty years before, so the Syren was the last of New Quay's big ships.

Captain Edward Jones' last voyages were made to Australia and the West Coast of South America: the latter among the most dangerous ever undertaken in sailing ships because of the treacherous coast and the violent storms experienced there except in the southern summer. Days spent taking in sail with frostbitten fingers and cracked and bloody hands rubbed raw by the soaked and salty rigging, fighting the spiralling winds for weeks on end until some captains despaired of ever rounding the Horn and ran for Australia, or limped back to Montevideo for repairs. There was the perpetual threat of Antarctic icebergs, or of being pooped by the vast seas which churn at the end of the world. These were all too common experiences off the Horn. And once safely past, their destinations, the nitrate ports of Chile or the guano islands off Peru, were considered by those who knew them to be the most desolate places on earth: "towns like Talcahuano and Antofogasta have a bleakly primitive look. With their unpaved streets lined with shops and houses clustered together on high wooden sidewalks they could well have served for models of frontier towns in the wild and woolly West... but the most unpopular places on the West coast were the guano islands. Guano, the product of centuries of bird droppings and widely used for fertiliser at that time, was broken down by Chinese coolies in a climate of dreadful heat, the stench was appalling. The stuff was sent down canvas chutes to waiting launches and consequently loading the cargo was a filthy task and as most of the nitrate centres had exposed roadstead and strong northerly winds, conditions were very dangerous". (24) Yet year after year sailors endured the hard life.

Captain Jones' new command was the iron barque Adventurer, 716 tons, built in Glasgow in 1875 by

Dobie & Co, and owned by Doward, Dixon & Co of Liverpool. She was typical of the larger vessels now being built in metal to compete with steamers for declining freights. Surviving Crew Agreements show that she was bound for Brisbane from New York in August 1889. Her crew were a mixed bunch: a young First Mate of 25 from Liverpool, a Scottish Second Mate aged 41; four English hands, five Scandinavians, a Chilean and two Germans. Her normal complement was considered to be ten or eleven and those above that number were classified as extra hands, but she generally carried fourteen or fifteen crew: besides the mates and cook and steward, there was a carpenter/AB, six other ABs and three boys on this occasion as well as an apprentice. She was in Brisbane on 20th December 1889 and left for Newcastle, New South Wales, on 9th January to load coal for Mollendo in Peru. She crossed the Pacific in 73 days and after discharging her cargo proceeded to Taltal in Chile to load a cargo of nitrates. Here the articles record the committal of two of her crew, Alfred Wickstrom, the carpenter, and William Slater, one of the boys, to prison, their offence not being named, but it must have been serious since the average misdemeanour: drunkenness or striking an officer was punishable by a fine of 5/- and general dissatisfaction was dealt with by discharging the culprit. Alfred Wickstrom was left his pay of over £40; the boy had only £1/3/6. On the Adventurer the Mate received £6/5/- a month. 2nd Mate £4; the Carpenter £5 and the Cook and Steward £4/15/-; the ABs £3, Ordinary Seamen £2 and boys 10/-. Wickstrom and Slater were not replaced and the Adventurer left Taltal on 21st June 1890, making the passage to Hamburg in 124 days.

She returned to Liverpool then to collect another cargo for Valparaiso. This time she had a Welsh mate Thomas Roberts of Caernarfon, formerly on the Glanivor and the 2nd mate was another Welshman, from Llannon, Cardiganshire, E M Evans. The outward voyage to Valparaiso took 98 days. Two men deserted there and another at Coquimbo where the Adventurer called briefly on 22nd April 1891 before sailing to Talcahuano to load nitrates, she was there two and a half months and perhaps this prospect led to the desertions. She left on 6th August and was back in Plymouth in 101 days for orders: i.e. instructions for the delivery of the cargo, as in their long absence other deals might have been arranged.

The captain was only in his late forties but the last photograph of him taken aboard the Adventurer (see Welsh Sail) makes him appear much older. He set out again for Valparaiso on 9th January, 1892. Thomas Roberts was still First Mate and Ellis C Ellis, also of Caernarfon was 2nd Mate. Some of the crew of the previous voyage signed on again, including William Theophile, the German carpenter. Their places of origin were as diverse as before: Antwerp, Rotterdam, Norway, the Isle of Man and Greece, but most gave their addresses, appearing for the first time in the articles, as Liverpool lodging-houses. Also in the crew was Edward's wife's nephew, Thomas Jones, aged 19, an Able Seaman. There were fourteen crew altogether and the apprentice, William Kitto Giddings, who had joined the Adventurer in 1889. One of the New Quay boys supposed to accompany Thomas Jones fell sick and young John Thomas Evans must have reckoned himself lucky when the news came, many months later. The Adventurer rounded the Horn safely and after discharging her cargo at Valparaiso, went on across the Pacific to Newcastle which she reached in November 1892. Here the Manxmen deserted: as one of these, John Quayle, had signed on again after the previous voyage, it was unlikely that he disliked his berth, so it is possible they fell prey to the notorious Newcastle crimps, they too had a lucky escape. The Adventurer returned to Taltal with her cargo of coal and then sailed in ballast from Taltal to Talcahuano on 13th March 1893. She was never seen again although she was not presumed lost for six months. Two men had joined her in Taltal: J Jones and J Northcote, aged 22 and 23, but though the consuls in the various ports searched diligently up and down the coast, no further details were available and their place of origin was marked "unknown" in the report of the loss.

So Edward Jones could not attend his son's wedding later that year: the boy who had sailed with him in the Syren was now on the way up the ladder with the Ropner shipping firm, in steam; seventeen years later, however, his grandson and namesake was rounding the Horn in the barque Madagascar. On 1st November 1909 he wrote home to his mother from Caleta Bueno: "There are eight sailing ships here now and four of them will sail about the same time for the Channel for orders viz Alsterdam, Madagascar, Admiral Troude and Naiad". For New Quay boys the world of sail was still a small one.: "There is a Welsh barque here called the Caradog and she belongs to Aberystwyth; there's only one Welshman aboard and that's the skipper, he comes from

Aberayron". On the Naiad was John Richard Davies, Arba, New Quay: "he comes over to the Madagascar every Sunday morning and then I go over with him in the afternoon and get a fine cup of tea and some duff". J R Davies had left New Quay more recently than Eddie Jones and was able to give him news of his younger brothers and his school friends. At Valparaiso Eddie had seen another New Quay man, Gwyn Phillips, who was First Mate on a sailing ship. He ended "We have now finished loading all except one lighter about 400 bags and we will sail in about a week's time. We are bound for Plymouth for orders and the old man thinks that she will go to Ardrossan to discharge. It will take us between 100 and 120 days to get home. Last voyage she took 139 days to Plymouth and most of the time she had head winds".

Eddie Jones and J R Davies were among the last young men in New Quay in sail; both made their later careers in steam, Eddie with Shell and J R Davies with the Blue Funnel Line. Only the previous year the Carnedd Llewelyn, under the command of Captain Thomas Evans, New Quay, with several New Quay men and boys among her crew, including the mate Evan James, (brother of Captain John James who was lost mysteriously off the Resolven) (25); Captain Evans own son, Percy aged 15, and another fifteen year old, Philip Wallace James, had been lost off Cape Horn, probably in collision with one of the vast icebergs which drifted up from Antarctica. The master of the Cognati, formerly the Ben Voirlich, collided with an iceberg, but the ship managed to free herself and when she reached Montevideo for repairs she reported seeing "a lot of wreckage and boats adrift in the ice". At this time twelve ships were overdue which included the Carnedd Llewelyn and none were ever heard of again. "Rather unusually," wrote Alan Villiers, "a search was organised for possible survivors from these ships... around the coasts of Tierra del Fuego and some of the Patagonian islands. Nothing was seen of them, though from time to time odd pieces of wreckage... were found and once, at least, some skeletons beside a heap of mussel shells". (26)

A happier voyage to Valparaiso is commemorated in the following shanty:

BOUND AWAY IN THE DOUNE CASTLE
(words by J Townsend)
On the 14th of January from Shields town we sailed
In a barque hailed from Glasgow the Doune Castle
was named
They bid us farewell as along we did go
Bound away in the Doune Castle to Valparaiso.

Now we are bowling through the old Tyne Dock
The lads and the lasses on the pier head did flock
They gave us three cheers as away we did go
Bound away in Doune Castle to Valparaiso.

So now we are laying in the old River Tyne
All waiting for the Sailor Boy to tow us to sea
He will tow us across the bar where the old
Tyne does flow
Bound away in the Doune Castle to Valparaiso.

So now we are sailing down along the Kentish shore
All waiting to put the old pilot ashore
We will put him on shore and away we will go
Bound away in Doune Castle to Valparaiso.

We landed our Pilot in the famed Isle of Wight
To see that fine town twas a beautiful sight
Then we braced up our yards and away we did go
Bound away in Doune Castle to Valparaiso

So now my boys we are crossing the line
Poor old Neptune comes on board in good time
He shaved all our lads and our passenger also
Bound away in Doune Castle to Valparaiso.

In the year 87 while passing the Plate
Our ship she was put in a terrible state
We lost all our sails both aloft and below
Bound away in Doune Castle to Valparaiso.

In the same year I sing of a Good Friday morn
Our topsail yards went as the day it did dawn
We encountered a storm which made our ship go
To our port of discharge called Valparaiso.

On the ...of April we rounded Cape Horn
The wind did blow fresh as the day it did dawn
We left it behind us to see it once more
When we are homeward bound to old England's shore.

So now my boys our passage is o'er
We sailed into port as we oft done before
Our sails we furled and our anchors let go
In that beautiful harbour called Valparaiso.

Sea Shanties were sung on most sailing ships when working at the capstan and the pump, hoisting the anchor and in larger vessels to haul tight the sails. There were capstan or windlass shanties, fore sheet shanties, each one recognised as appropriate for a particularly tough job of work. Stan Hugill of Aberdyfi, who collected Shanties from the Seven Seas, traced their development through the ages from the yells of the early hauling and heaving songs to the rather tuneless short hauls and sweating-up songs: "Cheerly Man, Boney, Handy Me Boys" to the familiar lilt of "Blow the Man down" and "Shenandoah" and "Rio". Sailors were fond of music and nearly every crew contained some member with a musical instrument, perhaps a fiddle, or more likely a 'squeeze-box', a concertina. Songs were often composed about their own ships when off-watch and these songs too are recognised by a special name: "fore-bitters the Yankees call them" or "main-hatch songs", because it was there the sailors foregathered off-duty in fair weather. (27)

Captain Jones, Adpar, New Quay, as mentioned earlier, commanded the Doune Castle and wrote down the words of the song commemorating her voyages to South America. The Doune Castle, like the Osaka, was a former tea-clipper and under the command of Captain Erskine had raced home from Shanghai in 1872 in 123 days, only one day longer than the Cutty Sark.

The Doune Castle reached her destination safely on this occasion as the cheerful ballad relates but other poetical effusions recall sadder occasions, like the Welsh poem illustrated here, recording the loss of the Sylph.

CAN NEWYDD,

A GYFANSODDWYD AR YR ACHLYSUR GALARUS O

LONG-DDRYLLIAD

Y SCHOONER SYLPH, CEI-NEWYDD,

YN NGHYD A

Saith o Forwyr, heblaw amryw ereill, a gollodd eu bywydau yn yspaid y Gauaf hwnw.

GAN DANIEL JONES, DILLEDYDD.

HOLL dadau a mamau gofidus,
A'r gweddwon rho'wch osteg i'm cân,
Mae'r hanes difrifol a roddaf
Bron rhwystro fy awen yn lân;
Ond etto ymdrechaf trwy ddagrau,
Er cymmaint y rhwystrau y sydd,
Mae Llywydd y gwyntoedd a'r moroedd
Yn abl fy nghynnal bob dydd.

Poem on the loss of the schooner *Sylph* of New Quay, with 7 sailors and others who lost their lives during that winter, 1850. The *Sylph* was launched in 1845 and traded to Archangel for hemp. Courtesy of Mrs Lilwen Lewis.

CHAPTER VIII

"The old order changeth, yielding place to new..." (1) The Decline of the Port

Between 1850 and 1880 forty-two New Quay-owned vessels were lost at sea, in ten cases with most of their crews. This was not unusual. In 1854 the Welsh newspaper Y Wasg, then published in Aberystwyth, recorded that 1,115 ships had been wrecked on the coast of Britain alone in the past year, 500 being completely written off. But thirty-four of New Quay's losses took place over the fifteen years from 1865 to 1880. This must have had a serious effect upon the prosperity of the shipbuilding industry and on those who managed the vessels. One of the worst years for losses lies outside this period: in 1887 a further six vessels were lost. They were covered by insurance but the New Quay Mutual Ship Insurance Society founded in the 1850s must have found it hard to cope with the succession of losses and, in fact, E Beynon Davies, in his history of New Quay, printed in 1913, suggests that they were unable to meet their obligations. Some of those lost were older vessels, small sloops and coasters which had spent thirty years and more at sea: the 50 ton sloop Linnet was seventy years in the coasting trade before her final shipwreck on Lavan Sands in November 1890, but others represented a much greater loss of investment, like the schooner Ceretica, already mentioned, lost in 1851, less than two years after her launch; and the brig Triton, launched in 1867 at Cei Bach and lost at Martinique in 1870, and the Maggie Phillips, a 165 ton brigantine, built by Evan Daniel in 1878 and wrecked on the coast of Brazil, sixty miles to the north of the port of Rio Grande del Sol on 15th June 1885. Providentially the crew was saved. The loss of the Maggie Phillips was a great blow to New Quay shareholders at a time when they were already feeling the pinch of declining freights for sailing vessels. Some of the new, large Canadian vessels were frequently lost within a few years of their purchase, like the Annie Ramsay, bought in 1863 and lost in 1867, or the Maggie Cummins, a 293 ton brig, bought in 1875 and lost off Mexico in 1880, though these were perhaps insured elsewhere.

It is rare for details of ship losses at sea to survive, since there are seldom witnesses, but some of the brig Hetty Ellen's last hours afloat were described by her would-be rescuers. On 2nd November 1881 the Hetty Ellen sailed from Malpeque for the Bristol Channel with a cargo of oats and deal boards. She was then 21 years old; since her launching in Llanelli by James Bevans in 1860, she had had an active career under three New Quay masters: David Davies, John Davies and Thomas Evans. While under the command of David Davies in 1861, she was chartered at Glasgow to load the stores for the Zambezi expedition of David Livingstone, the famous explorer, including the unassembled twin screw iron river steamer, the Lady Nyasa. In her lifetime the Hetty Ellen carried cargoes to Bahia, Baltimore, Berbice, Bilbao, Constantinople, Demerara, East London, Havana, Jamaica, Pernambuco, Pomeran, Prince Edward Island, Rio de Janeiro, Rosario, Trieste and Trinidad. The economical prose of the Log of the City of Halifax recorded her death-throes on that last voyage from Prince Edward Island: "on 27th November 1881 in latitude 47 degrees N longitude 35 degrees W fell in with Brig Hetty Ellen from PEI bound East, with rudder gone, maintopsailyard carried away, sails flying in ribbons, bulwarks stove in; signalled to us not to leave them; hove to, trying to take off the crew in the morning while blowing very hard, but gale sprang up, which lasted 36 hours, and we then searched a whole day for the vessel but could find nothing of her." (2)

Life at sea which brought so much prosperity for families once condemned to a life of hard agricultural labour or poorly paid craft, was a good deal more dangerous than labouring and the prosperity had to be off-set against the grievous personal tragedies which often accompanied it. Walking through the graveyards around New Quay church and Maen-y-groes chapel, where primroses blow in spring on the green banks, one is made strongly aware of this: it seems that there is scarcely a stone which does not record the death of a member of the family in foreign parts, frequently more than one and many were lost in Cardigan Bay or the Irish Sea. To take just one example, John Phillips, son of William Phillips (a labourer, who lived at Parc, New Quay, later Park Street and survived to the age of 84), was lost at sea as master of the Ellen of New Quay, near "Saltees" on a voyage from Porthcawl to Skibbereen (Ireland), in 1880; his brother David had been drowned on a voyage from Pomeran, South America to Liverpool, in January 1865. I have recorded over 150 deaths at sea or in foreign ports from local graveyards, between 1850 and 1914.

In 1841 so many widows occupied houses in one street in New Quay that the Census enumerator wrote it down by its local nickname Widow Street (White Street now). There were Friendly Societies which assisted widows and orphans and paid for members' funerals as well and most people probably belonged to one of these. The steel cashbox of the Gomer Friendly Society has been preserved (in the possession of the late George Lister when I was shown it) and although most of its contents had long vanished, a scrap of a receipt survived: "From the Gomer Friendly Society the sum of £11/3/6 being the funeral fee due after the death of my beloved husband Capt. Evans of the Lettice Catherine. Given under my hand this 15th day of May 1867." The Lettice Catherine had been wrecked that year at Bahia Blanca. Another Friendly Society was "The Prince of Wales", this met, not at the later public-house of that name as might have been expected, but at the Castle Inn, half way up Church Street, according to its printed rules. These Friendly Societies were strictly controlled by law to safeguard the funds entrusted to them, every member paying a fixed sum regularly against the day when they would surely need it. Basil Greenhill has recorded: "Of British merchant shipmasters generally during the years 1835-1848 less than two-thirds died natural deaths and nearly a quarter lost their lives with their ships"; local gravestones tell a similar tale. But they continued to go to sea from New Quay for the next hundred years and more and many did survive to sit on fine mornings, in their retirement, at Cnwc-y-Glap, overlooking the Pier, reminiscing about New Quay's great days.

The building and re-building of ever larger chapels and the construction of the Patent Slip had all been positive, forward-looking measures which suggested great confidence in the future of New Quay in the 1860s, but in that very decade the coming of steam power was a threat to New Quay's enterprise. The Aberaeron Steam Navigation Company Ltd was founded in September 1863 and the railway from Shrewsbury reached Aberystwyth in 1864; subsequently a considerable decline was noticed in the record of ships entering and leaving Aberystwyth Harbour. The railway, the steamship and eventually the motor-lorry, were to spell the death-knell of the coasting trade and the large windjammer and steamship did the same to the deepwater trade of the smaller sailing vessel. New Quay's prosperity had been founded on these small sailing vessels: what could the people do when they were no longer an economic proposition? As I wrote in an earlier account of shipbuilding here: "That this small place could have conceived and maintained such a large fleet of ships, keeping them on deep water with stubborn determination virtually to the end of its days as an active port, is a tribute to the people's energy and ambition." (3) And they continued to manifest the same qualities in their efforts to keep the port open and not to dwindle into a "watering-place" or holiday resort to use the more modern term, though lodging houses appear for the first time in the 1881 Census, ironically at Brongwyn Street, once the home of the shipwrights.

Aberaeron had never had quite the scale of investment in sailing ships that New Quay had, building only about a quarter of the number launched in New Quay, so it was natural that she should consider steam ships at an earlier stage. But when the Steam Navigation Company was floated, some eight prescient New Quay investors are recorded, including several New Quay merchants: David James, Evan Timothy the younger, John Rees, William Jones, John Jones sail-maker, John Patrick of the Black Lion Inn, Captain David Evans, master of the schooner Confidence, a Mediterranean trader and David Jones, Derw Cottage, New Quay. Between them they owned 15 shares in the steamship Prince Cadwgan, commissioned from a Glasgow firm at a cost of £4,000. (4) The company did well, although repairs consumed a large proportion of the profits and it was soon after the fitting of a new boiler and engine that the Prince Cadwgan struck Crow Rocks off the Pembrokeshire coast and sank. The company had to be wound up and as few shares had changed hands the original shareholders bore the entire burden of the loss. However, a new company was launched almost immediately: the Aberaeron Steam Packet Company, which purchased the steamship Ianthe, built in Glasgow in 1873. "The prime mover of the new association was Thomas Davies, captain of the New Quay barque Prince Llewelyn, who owned a quarter of the new steamship and became managing director of the new company". (5) Within three years a dividend of sixteen per cent per annum was being paid.

Thomas Davies died in 1885 but the company flourished and another steamer, the Norseman was bought in 1894. The Ianthe was sold in 1895 and replaced by the Telephone and until after World War I both steamers brought in cargoes of general goods to New Quay, the Norseman from Bristol, the Telephone from Liverpool though by then the Aberaeron Company had been wound up as it could not stand the competition from the railroad which reached Aberaeron from Llandysul in 1911 and the vessels were owned by Bristol and Liverpool merchants.

By the 1880s tolls were falling in New Quay harbour and in 1883 the tolls were not let at auction; and the last dated entry in the Harbour Company's book, on 22nd October 1884, indicates a problem which was to plague the harbour increasingly: tenders were to be sought for dredging the harbour as sand was silting it up so badly. Dividends had fallen to half the amount paid in the 1850s.

The yard at the Patent Slip had continued to make a steady profit in the 1870s despite an incessant stream of outgoings. In some years there seems to have been a profit of £600. In 1880 the accounts still looked quite healthy: disbursements were £200 and the income amounted to over £600. However, the demand for repairs seems to have declined quite sharply thereafter and by 1882/3 the income was £131/10/3½ against outgoings of £45, though the latter figure did not include the salaries of the Company's officials. In these years, the vessels worked on include the Emrys, the Pheasant, the Ellen Ann, the Nymph, the Pacific, the U'Larsing, the

LIST OF APPROXIMATE SAILINGS.

The Liverpool & Menai Straits Steam Ship Co. Ltd.,
1912.

. . . REGULAR . . .
Steam Communication Between LIVERPOOL,

ABERAYRON, NEW-QUAY, CARDIGAN & FISHGUARD.

"TELEPHONE" S.

(CAPTAIN ROBERTS),
Will (weather and other circumstances permitting) leave West Side **TRAFALGAR LOCK,**
LIVERPOOL, for **the above Ports,** as follows:—

For ABERAYRON and NEW-QUAY.			For CARDIGAN and FISHGUARD.		
Monday ...	January	15th.	Friday ...	January	5th.
Tuesday ...	„	30th.	Saturday ...	„	20th.
Wednesday ...	February	14th.	Saturday ...	February	3rd.
Wednesday ...	„	28th.	Monday ...	„	19th.
Saturday ...	March	16th.	Monday ...	March	4th.
Thursday ...	„	28th.	Wednesday ...	„	20th.
Saturday ...	April	13th.	Tuesday ...	April	2nd.
Saturday ...	„	27th.	Wednesday ...	„	17th.
Saturday ...	May	11th.	Wednesday ...	May	1st.
Saturday ...	„	25th.	Thursday ...	„	16th.
Monday ...	June	10th.	Thursday ...	„	30th.
Monday ...	„	24th.	Saturday ...	June	15th.
			Saturday ...	„	29th.

Cargo received up to 5 p.m. on day of Sailing.
A limited number of passengers carried. Particulars to be had on board.

FOR CONDITIONS OF CARRIAGE SEE BACK HEREOF.

For Rates and other particulars, apply to—
AGENTS:—**CAPT. JONES,**
"Telephone" Office, ABERAYRON
OR TO
Mr. E. P. JONES,
Aeron House, NEW-QUAY (Card.)
OR TO
W. YANDELL,
Agent "Telephone," CARDIGAN
OR TO
B. A. EVANS,
Agent "Telephone," FISHGUARD

or to

ROBERT OWEN,
28, Brunswick Street, LIVERPOOL.
(TELEPHONE Nos. 1557, 1576 Central)
Telegraphic Address: "MERION," Liverpool

Poster advertising sailings of the steamer SS Telephone between Liverpool and Aberayron, New Quay, Cardigan & Fishguard, 1912.

Antelope, the John James, the Ann Warren, the Ina Lass, the Agnes Cairns, the Dolphin and the Dreadnought; between 1886 and 1890 the entries grow sporadic: there are references to Capt. Davies, Commerce; Captain David Williams, John James; Captain Davies, Susanna Gwenllian; Captain David James, Argo & Ann; Captain Evans, Packet and the Albatross, a Llangrannog-owned vessel. The last entry on 30th August 1890 relates to Daniel Jones "for two boats".

Two weeks later, an Extraordinary General Meeting of the members of the New Quay Patent Slip Company was announced: to be held at their Registered Office at Glyn Square on the last day of the month to wind up the company voluntarily and appoint a liquidator; a task which finally devolved on Joshua Jones. Evan Timothy the younger and Evan Phillips were dead; Evan Phillips' son was a shipbroker in Swansea. They were all old men, Joshua in his 70s. "For a few brief years they were at the heart of a great burst of enterprise and outward-looking activity... then they vanished like monuments made of snow", (6) wrote Basil Greenhill of the men of Prince Edward Island and so it was in New Quay. Evan Daniel, her last shipbuilder, died the same year. It was the end of an era.

Yet the port went down fighting. In 1899 a New Quay Development Company was formed in an effort to halt the decline. In June that year, a Petition was addressed to the Right Honourable Charles T Ritchie, MP, the President of the Board of Trade, Whitehall, London. (7) "The Humble Petition of the undersigned being tradesmen, Merchants and Ship owners, resident at New

Quay in the parish of Llanllwchaearn in the county of Cardigan respectfully sheweth" is its preamble. The gist of the petition is a serious complaint against the directors of the Harbour Company because the harbour has become so silted up in recent years that few vessels of any size can use it. "The direct loss to the trade of the district consequent on the unnavigable state of the Harbour is, in the opinion of your Petitioners, so great as to deserve the direct and most serious attention of your honourable Board". They refer to the inability of the Norseman to come alongside the discharging slip even at high tide and having to run up on to the foreshore, and often even only half a cargo could be brought in because of the problems of discharging and "Nevertheless the Harbour Company continue to levy on all goods and ships heavier rates and tonnage duties than are levied by any other Harbour Company in the United Kingdom, Your petitioners most earnestly affirm that this state of things is cruelly unjust to the ship owners and trades people of New Quay and most seriously menacing to the very existence of this once industrious and prosperous town".

Even the few small coasting vessels which New Quay still possessed "are invariably forced to lie in the mouth of the harbour for periods varying in length from 5 to 14 days waiting for tides to come alongside the discharging wharf". At this time, most of New Quay's vessels had been lost or sold away, those still afloat included the schooners Jane & Mary, built in 1842, the John & Mary built in 1848, the Ann Warren, 1857, the Equity, 1858, the Pacific, 1859, the little Thomas & Sons and the Utopia, 1860, the smack George Evans, now ketch-rigged, 1862; the schooners Clarita, 1870 and the Ina

SS Norseman discharging cargo on the beach with the pier and in the background. Author's collection.

Lass, 1871, the sloop Eliza Anne, 1877 and two recently acquired ketches, the Main and the Fleetwing, purchased in 1894. John Davies, Albion, was still managing the Dreadnought, launched in 1866, which continued in the South American trade until her loss three years later, but she was no longer based here.

It was all the more galling in that there was an opportunity for New Quay to have an export trade in stone which was being thwarted, as the Committee, saw it, by the Harbour Company's intransigence. "There is at New Quay," the Petition continued, "an exceedingly large Quarry of building or curbing stones proved by experts to be of excellent quality, capable of commanding a free and ready market. On the 10th day of March this year (1899) a strong deputation appointed by an enthusiastic public meeting held at New Quay, interviewed the directors of the New Quay Harbour Company on the subject of the development of the Vrondolay (sic) Quarry and in response to their appeal received terms which your Petitioners regard as utterly unjust and impracticable and which the Owners of the said Quarry could not for a moment entertain... your petitioners are convinced that it is the settled purpose of the owner of Vrondolay Quarry when proper Harbour facilities have been secured to them to work his large property on a greatly extended scale, employing about 200 hands and eventually a still larger number." Although the figures for future employment may have been somewhat exaggerated, the petitioners were right in thinking that this would have been a profitable venture for New Quay. The tiny port of Porthgain in Pembrokeshire had at this time and would have until

1931 a very successful export business in crushed stone and up to the twenties "there was a constant activity in the harbour both sailing and steam vessels loading and some sixty or seventy men constantly employed." (8)

In addition, the traditional argument in favour of New Quay as a harbour of asylum was revived. The wreck of the Bronwen eight years before was still a vivid memory in the town although as the Bronwen struck the coast near Target Rock by the Quarry (9), the case of the trawler Beatrice of Pwllheli, in 1896, was more germane to their thesis. "This vessel had been riding at anchor during low water in the mouth of the harbour when a storm arose and drove her up on the beach where she received considerable damage. A splendid effort was made to take the lifeboat to the rescue of the crew but the tide being out the lifeboat became immovably fixed in the sands where it remained until it was floated away by the next tide". Only the previous year there had been a similar occurrence with the Aberystwyth trawler ICW. It was also stated that the Aberaeron Steam Packet Company and a number of local trades people were refusing to pay Harbour dues.

There appears to have been no response to the petition and in November 1899 an effort was made to purchase the shares of the Harbour Company as it was felt public ownership would result in the improvement of commercial prospects in the town. Hopes were now pinned on another petition to the Treasury regarding the construction of a Light Railway to New Quay. It was headed:

The Petition of the Landowners, Farmers and Inhabitants of the several parishes of New Quay,

Llanllwchaearn, Llanina, Henfynyw, Cydplwyf, Llanarth, Llandysiliogogo, Llangranog, Penbryn, Blaenporth, Bettws Evan, Troedyraur, Llangunllo and Brongwyn in the County of Cardigan..." showing that the New Quay Committee had canvassed to some purpose in neighbouring districts. The petitioners "respectfully" suggested several possible routes for the projected railway:

"1 From Newcastle Emlyn via Gogerddan Arms and Brynhoffnant to New Quay
2 From Henllan via Rhydlewis and Ffostrassol to New Quay
3 From Llandyssil through the Clettwr Valley and via Talgarreg to New Quay
4 From Llanybyther via Cribyn, Mydroilyn and Llanarth to New Quay."

These routes had been investigated carefully and the Petitioners were satisfied that the expenditure would be reasonable for an undertaking of this type and "It is also beyond question that it would be an enormous advantage to the whole agricultural population along the route of the said Railway". The Petition included the following Summary as evidence of the annual trade of the area to be served by the railway: see Plate 32.

It was hoped that the Treasury would, as it was entitled to do under the terms of the Light Railways Act of 1896, make a contribution from public funds towards the expense of the construction.

The Great Western railway were approached as well with the carrot of being offered "gratis, all the harbour

A Summary of the Annual Trade of the District served by the proposed ... Railway to New Quay ...

DISTRICTS	Coal & Culm.	Manure	Lime Bricks, & c.	Horses	Cattle	Sheep & Pigs	Poultry	Butter & Cheese	Other Farm Produce	Shop Goods	PASSENGERS
	Tons	*Tons*	*Tons*					*Tons*	*Tons*	*Tons*	
Cross Inn	520	151	497	55	390	1989	3927	27	78	590	670
Ffostrassol & Rhydlewis	2465		1027	193	1565	13244	12716	1556	162	2910	
Glynarthen	431	116	177		257	1660				700	
Brongest, including Troedyraur and part of Betws Evan	564	120	120	50	237	1492	2530	852			
Sarnau	306				97	436				100	
Brynhoffnant	123	34	136		236	579		107		309	
Llandysiliogogo... ...	164	63	75	18	131	497	211	5	6	211	
Tanygroes, Aberporth & Traethsaith	2000			60	240	1500	*Tons*	30	45	500	12710 } Day visitors
Llangranog	1720	100				1510	*15*	14	20	608	4900 } included
New Quay	3195	337	417							Freight -age to steamer £486	10412 & Day visitors at least 10,000

A summary of the annual Trade of the district served by the proposed railway to New Quay 1899.

rights". A rather patronising note was struck in one letter: "With your co-operation and influence we do not see therefore why the railway should not come to New Quay and immediately branch off to other towns such as Aberaeron to the north which is a most promising town, and Llangrannog to the south which also promises well." Ironically "the most promising town" got the railway instead, though not until 1911. (10) The Committee also emphasised that a railway would assist the sale of fish too though in their zeal there is a contradiction between this petition designed to show railway prospects in a favourable light and the former designed to show the Harbour Company as the villains of the piece: "the Harbour here affording facilities for landing at all states of the tides and weather"; whereas to the Board of Trade they had written: "In pursuance of the trade of Herring Fishing, the fishermen are compelled by the state of the Harbour to run the great risk of being caught during low water in the prevailing westerly and north westerly gales of Cardigan bay. In cases of this kind the fishermen are forced to take one of two courses, namely to face the fury of the gale in their small half-open boats or run them up on to the rocky beach".

A later petition to the Board of Trade reveals another volte-face: everyone has now joined forces; it is headed "The Humble Petition of the under-signed being members of the New Quay UDC (New Quay became an Urban District in 1894), Directors of the New Quay Harbour Company, owners of land on the coast referred to herein, ship owners, merchants and tradesmen resident in New Quay... in the opinion of your

Petitioners it would be quite useless for the New Quay Harbour Company to expend any of their limited means in dredging the Harbour until effective means have been applied to prevent further erosion of the coast within the harbour limits". This, alas, remains a burning question to this day. It concludes like the earlier petition: "And your Petitioners will ever pray etc" as if it was addressed to Queen Elizabeth I and not a twentieth century Minister.

Although the railway did not materialise, the GWR continued to be bombarded with requests for at least a motor service between the railway terminus at Llandysul and New Quay. One of the pleas was that "The majority of the residents of New Quay belong to the sea-faring class and this necessitates frequent travelling by sailors and their families between seaports and their homes," another was that "three of the leading tradesmen pay annually an average of fifty pounds each in cartage from Llandysul, this being in addition to the general delivery by the regular carrier", and the Committee were disparaging about "our present antiquated and inconvenient method of travelling."

The carriers' carts of William Thomas and Dafydd Williams continued to ply for a few years longer: at least the arrival of the railway at Llandysul saved them the former twelve-hour journey to Carmarthen; the tri-weekly journey to Aberystwyth took four or five hours. The Mail too continued to be brought in on the smart Mail trap and donkeys' hooves and the rumble of their cartwheels continued to sound in the streets of New Quay as they delivered goods from house to house. In

1906, however, the GWR opened a bus service between Lampeter and Aberaeron and between Aberaeron and Aberystwyth and slowly the carriers' beat diminished: in the following year New Quay finally achieved its motor bus service to Llandysul and brought to an end the carriers' trade. The following verse was composed to commemorate the replacement of the wagonette drawn by 'Jack and Charlie':

Fi yw'r van fu'n cario bobol
I Llandysul yn amserol
Dychwel wnawn ymrig yn hwyrnos
Glongi-glonc gan drin bob achos
Nawr mae pethau wedi newid
Modur drewllyd red o Parcstryd
Crynwr yw, ni wyr am stori
A milgi dall yn difa Powltri.

I am the van which carried people
In timely fashion to Llandysul
Returning in the dusk of even
Chatting away on every topic
Now things have changed
A stinking motor runs from Park Street
A real shaker no pleasant chatter
A blind greyhound ravaging poultry.

Despite the occasional accident, by 1911, Mr John Thomas of Frondolau could write: "Motor vehicles having at present attained great efficiency and reliability I would respectfully pray that a trial of them be made in the Postal Service between New Quay and Llandysul." He had worked out the economics very carefully: "an

Dafydd Williams' carrier's cart, with Miss Maggie Brooks seated next to him, she lived in George Street, at the start of which this photograph was taken, probably by her father Shirley Brooks, a photographer in New Quay for many years at his George Street Studio.

average of only three passengers daily on Motor Mails" would at 3/- per passenger produce an annual revenue of £160." Soon that too was history. But Jack and Charlie, Brown, Polly and Captain were affectionately remembered for many years. The town's rubbish continued to be collected by horse and cart until 1950 and when Bess retired the Rev David Pugh preached a sermon dedicated to her sturdy service. She was not quite the last whose hooves sounded in New Quay's streets since for a time Mr Griff Thomas delivered meat in his smart yellow-painted cart.

The economic miracle was over and there would not be another for New Quay: the petitions were a last-ditch

This little donkey cart photographed in Lewis Terrace, belonged to the Black Lion and was typical of those used to make deliveries in the town. Authors collection.

stand. In future, apart from her men folk still serving in great numbers at sea in other ports' ships, the town would have to depend once more upon fishing and the increasing seasonal trade provided by visitors. Already in 1885, only three years after the launch of the last vessel at Cei Bach, a visitor was writing in The Christian World: "I have discovered Ultima Thule". The author raved over the unspoilt peace of the Cardiganshire coast with no railway at all south of Aberystwyth: "For miles before we turned out of the Cardigan road we had seen our destination, a little town white in the bright sunshine, built along the steep sides of a shimmering bay. And presently the lanes ended and the horses were scrambling up what seemed like the side of a house into the street (this was Brongwyn Street). We had arrived... the little town was the quaintest, most picturesque one could wish to see... each cottage had its garden... no bands, no minstrels... no dressed windows in the place. All was quiet, leisurely, old-fashioned... the blossoms were unmatched for size and colour." The visitor was impressed with the "delightful foreignness" of hearing Welsh spoken everywhere and with the enthusiasm with which church and chapel services were attended. He concluded "for many years to come I think it will remain a refuge for weary workers who love the hills and the sea and the wild lanes, but who flee from the life of the lodging-house and the voices of the Christy Minstrels."

Three years later, in the Cheltenham Examiner, New Quay had some more free publicity from another delighted visitor, who had travelled on the railway to Llanydsul: "It is when you leave the iron way and are mounted on top of the Llandysul and New Quay 'bus that your enjoyment really begins.“ this was of course the carrier’s cart. “Mr Thomas our driver who knows the history of the owner of every field we pass” was “the cheeriest of companions.” Walking the glorious cliffs, bathing “free of cost”, trips on “pleasure boats” from the beach to the Red Cask which marked Llanina Point or further down the coast to Birds’ Rock or through the mysterious “double-headed cave” nearby, were the main attractions.

These extracts are quoted in what is probably the first printed Guide to New Quay: Being a short description of New Quay as a Watering-place, which was printed in Lampeter at the Welsh Press in 1895, by an anonymous author: JL. There are references still to “numerous coasters... frequently coming in and going out” and to the fortnightly calls of the Steamship Ianthe bringing goods from Bristol but once-busy Cei Bach was “a small and dilapidated village of half-a-dozen houses; this is a favourite picnicking rendezvous. The beach is sandy and the surroundings highly interested.” (sic) He makes no mention of Siani Bob Man, who if not then, soon after became one of the attractions of visiting Cei Bach. She shared her cottage on the beach with her hens and cockerel, dyeing her eggs brown with tea to make them more attractive for sale and earned her nickname - she was baptised Jane Leonard - from her custom of patrolling the countryside, visiting various farms, where she was always made welcome and given a present of food. At her cottage she would often entertain tourists by singing to them and telling fortunes. Although she was in receipt of only 2/- a week from the Poor Law Union, she lived very frugally and on her death in 1917

£100 was found in a box beneath the bed, with a note saying it was to be given to Aberaeron Hospital.

The Coastguards "whose weekly shooting and drilling practices delight the visitors", the former at Target Rock, were another attraction and so was the lifeboat house with tours taken by the Chief Coxwain. "The natives are considered refined, brave, industrious and hardy... None are more closely connected with National and Patriotic feelings" as they were indeed to reveal on many occasions in the harsher future, but the tumult of war seemed far removed from those golden summers. "Rumour has it, that taking into account the number of its population, New Quay has probably produced more Master Mariners than any other seaside place in the Principality. They are strict Sabbatarians and a high moral tone pervades the whole place." This was written several years before the great Revival of 1904 was sparked off in New Quay. (11)

Visitors were also assured that it was remarkably healthy: "the annual death-rate of the district (frequently only ten per thousand) is one of the lowest in the Kingdom." Rather ironically, in view of the still high death-toll among the younger inhabitants, it was recommended "to those who have a tendency to consumption". But JL assured his readers: "Parties have been known to leave many pounds heavier in weight" and "zymotic diseases are almost unknown."

The Reading Room founded by Charles Longcroft and David Evans, forty years before, was still open and now also contained "Lloyds Lending Library" with books costing borrowers a penny or tuppence or three pence a week, depending on the original price of the book. The authors whose works were then available included Alexandre Dumas, Charles Dickens, Thomas Carlyle and Wilkie Collins as well as many now forgotten novelists like Edna Lyall and Samuel Lover.

"Excellent accommodation both at Hotels and Private Houses is obtainable and this at a comparatively low figure. Apartments being so abundant here, the tastes and pockets of all classes of visitors can be suited... the landlady will provide all food to order." Right up until the 1960s most people provided bed and breakfast accommodation for summer visitors, who returned year after year to their favourite guest-house, and to provide accommodation some families even slept in garden sheds. Unfortunately, thereafter, the trend came for purchasing summer-houses and today you find streets of well-maintained houses which are nevertheless empty for the greater part of the year and the permanent population has declined to 700. From the 1950s too came the development of the vast caravan sites which now surround New Quay.

But these trends were as yet undreamt of in the 1890s though the little guidebook contains several photographs one of which shows the pier as crowded in summer as it is today. Most of the photographs were taken by John Price, who had a studio at 11 Lewis Terrace. The guidebook closed with the pious hope that the railway might never come to overwhelm New Quay with "the fashionable world". It would take the motor-car to do that. But even then, visitors were arriving in thousands, as the summary of annual trade revealed, the seaside holiday was becoming an established custom. New Quay attracted many colliers from South Wales who stayed at Brongwyn Street and Rock Street (sharing rooms for 1/- a night) and enchanted English visitors (who generally stayed in High Terrace and Pengeulan) with their impromptu choirs on the pier head in the evening. Among the colliers in 1882, was a young man named David Davies from Abercanaid, near Merthyr Tudfil. During his summer holiday at New Quay he met and fell in love with Jennie Davies, daughter of Capt. Davies, Caitloch and they eloped in December that year. Although at first, Jennie's family felt he was not a suitable match, one day they were to be very proud of their son-in-law. Self-educated, he became the manager of the Britannia colliery, and internationally renowned for his geological researches in the South Wales Coal-fields and his collection can be seen today at the National Museum of Wales. (12)

A golf-course was opened in 1914 and the summer celebration of the Regatta was then associated with the newly-introduced Carnival: races taking place in the morning and a colourful procession around New Quay in the afternoon with a Fancy dress Ball that night. The little Park on the seafront was created to mark the coronation of King George V, replacing the earlier coal yard, which by then was considered to detract from the appearance of the new 'watering-place'. The Regatta was however cancelled in 1914, owing to the outbreak of war. I have written an account of New Quay's service and sacrifice in a booklet published by Ceredigion Museum. (13) Belgian refugees replaced holiday makers and many retained lifelong links with their hosts. The

Memorial Hall erected after World War I provided a larger venue for entertainments and eventually a cinema, although when the silent film "Torn Sails" was partly filmed here in 1920, the nearest cinema was in Aberaeron. "Torn Sails" was based on the novel of the same name by Allen Raine. This was the pseudonym of Mrs Anne Adeliza Puddicombe, born in 1836 in Newcastle Emlyn, daughter of Benjamin Evans, a solicitor, and great-grand-daughter of David Davies, Castellhywel. She spent many childhood holidays at Tresaith and was married in 1872 at Penbryn Church to Beynon Puddicombe, a foreign correspondent for Smith's Bank. Her first published story was Ynysoer, written in English, for which she shared the prize for the best serial story in Welsh or English characteristic of Welsh life, at the National Eisteddfod in 1894. This was eventually published as Where Billows Roll. It was set in Tresaith and Llangrannog and eventually sold over 300,000 copies. Her second book was Torn Sails also set in Tresaith under the name of Mwntseison and tells the story of Hugh Morgan who owns the sail making business on which the village depends. It is a story of jealousy and unrequited love, the sail-loft being destroyed by Gwen, the villainess of the story. Despite its melodramatic qualities it was also an enormous success and twelve years after Allen Raine's death, was filmed by the Ideal Film Company. The film has not survived but stills from it can be seen at the Heritage Centre, along with shots from the 1954 film "The Constant Husband" for which the famous star, Rex Harrison, came to film at New Quay. Incidentally one of the most attractive things about this film for us locals are the opening shots where the director filmed our then fishing fleet under sail, the only record of it as far as I know with the Camellia, Deryn du, Salian, Enid tearing along. In 2007, a film based on a dramatic event in Dylan Thomas'life: "The Edge of Love", was filmed almost entirely in New Quay with many local people as extras. Dylan Thomas, the impecunious poet, spent part of World War II here and his radio script Quite Early One Morning was based on New Quay as was his more famous play Under Milk Wood. I wrote an account of New Quay in World War II, entitled One Village's War, to mark the 50th anniversary of the end of the war, in 1995.

Confirmation that New Quay changed very little between 1895and the late 1940s is provided by Walter Wilkinson, who wrote Puppets in Wales about his travels with a puppet theatre on a handcart: "with a charm which could have delighted George Borrow himself" as the Daily Telegraph said of an earlier book Vagabonds and Puppets. He brought his show to New Quay in the summer of 1947:

"New Quay Cardiganshire... is a trap, a cunning contrivance for inveigling travellers to ceasing their travels. You are tipped into it from the hills, as a fly is tipped into a jar of syrup; you come to an edge and over you go, down the slippery slope, through the three or four terraces of cottages on the hillside, by those narrow steep streets among the cottages, down to the hotel in the old sail maker's works, down to the jetty and the two or three boats jigging on the green water....

History has stood still or even gone backwards in New Quay. Time and the sea have nibbled at it: the sea has

Filming "Torn Sails" outside the Wellington Inn, in 1920. The summery clothes of the onlookers convey the holiday atmosphere though the eager crowd is obscuring the actual action which is taking place in the top right-hand corner. Author's Collection.

encroached, and where, as a child, you might have walked across the fields and among the cows, you now walk on wet sand. The meadows and all the daisies are obliterated by sand and sea...

The distinction of New Quay is that it has no railway station and does not exhibit itself on the hoardings claiming to be the sunniest, noisiest and most vulgar Bedlam of the West. Although it must live to a great extent on visitors, it has not yet obscured itself under all those horrible catch-penny aids to a fortnight's holiday. It has the merit of not being up-to-date; ... it would seem the last hundred years have hardly touched the place. The farm fields still come down to the town, and as you walk from the baker to the draper you can talk to a donkey and a horse, poking their heads over a fence into the street." Maisie the donkey was, as a matter of fact, never content with viewing the world from across a fence, but spent a great deal of her time ambling about the streets and calling at favoured houses for an apple, in those days when cars were far and few between.

"And New Quay has her indigenous population. Sea captains abound there; address any gentleman, not an obvious visitor, as a captain and you will be safe. After being in the Navy, or sailing cargoes for us all over the world, under the most difficult conditions, ruining their eyesight in peering through fog and driving snow, evading icebergs, sailing under air-raids and over submarines... it is very restful to think that they are safely anchored in such a haven, that they devote themselves to the placid game of bowls, rolling smooth round balls over smooth lawns - what a wonderful swing of the pendulum! What a just and perfect antidote to the too much raging sea and wartime..."

Walter Wilkinson, like the author of the 1895 guide-book, loved New Quay for what he saw as its unchanging quality, caught in a picturesque time-warp. Attractive though the picture is, it fails to recognise the lesson of history: if a place remains static, it dies; a living entity is constantly growing and evolving, adapting itself to changing circumstances as New Quay has done throughout its long history, seizing opportunities to develop and prosper. So it did throughout the 19th century and so it does today. There is perhaps now, as there is everywhere, when too much has been lost beyond recall, a greater appreciation of the value of our heritage but this goes hand in hand with enterprise.

Epilogue

New Quay developed from an essentially rural community of farmers, fishermen and craftsmen into a port with a flourishing shipbuilding industry, attracting investment and people, a microcosm of the vast Victorian ports like Manchester and Liverpool. For a few decades, New Quay was an important part of that phenomenal growth which made Britain the workshop of the world, the rapid spread of overseas trade to market her goods, which also led to colonisation and the development of a world-wide oceanic policy. H Moyse-Bartlett in his monograph From Sail to Steam comments: "From the time when its authority ceased any longer to meet with serious challenge during the Napoleonic War, British naval power assumed a position in world affairs far transcending the mere implications of what is known as foreign policy. In the suppression of slavery, the policing of the seas to stamp out piracy and the surveying and charting of distant waters, the Navy assumed an international role that came to be accepted by the British as part of its natural function. This could not have been accomplished had Britain failed to meet the growing demands made on her mercantile shipping after 1815. For naval power cannot be created by the mere voting of taxes; nor can it flourish except on the basis of a sound sea-faring tradition. This the Merchant navy provided during the 19th century on an expanding scale commensurate with the needs of a growing Empire. Historians have stressed at length the exploits of Tudor and Stuart seamen in the history of British expansion but similar influence on the growth of the Empire in more recent times is often too little regarded." (1)

Only a few souvenirs of the past remain today to show that New Quay was once a busy port with flourishing shipyards: a few worn wooden bollards and massive rusty flaking iron rings deeply embedded in quays and rocks to hold the big ships that have been firewood these many years. The Patent slip was broken up and sold for scrap and only the intervention of Mrs Lilwen Lewis saved some of the ancient chains from being carted away when the new Watersports Centre was built. The big sailrooms have become hotels and the smithies have vanished. Twenty years ago I wrote that only the ruined limekilns and vestiges of tumbled down cottages remained to remind one of the once flourishing community at Cei Bach, but the last of the limekilns has washed away although one can still trace the clom gable-end of Siani Bob Man's cottage. At Traethgwyn rows of caravans overlook the beach which once echoed to the clink of caulking mallets and the huzzas of the shipwrights as a completed vessel was launched. It was a great era in our history and should never be forgotten, but "time passes, time passes," as the Narrator said of the little town in Under Milk Wood and New Quay has embraced its destiny as a holiday resort with the fervour its people once showed for their ships.

References

Full source references are given in the Bibliography

Chapter I

1 Lewis, E A: The Port Book of Cardigan in Elizabethan and Stuart Times.
2 Davies, A S: Cardiganshire Salt Smugglers , pp312-313
3 Inglis-Jones, E: Peacocks in Paradise, p64
4 NLW Deposited MS 118
5 Davies, Noel: Prelude: The Red Dragon and the Rising Sun.
6 Jenkins, J Geraint: Herring Fishing in Wales, p15
7 NLW 14351A
8 See his will in S C Passmore: Llanllwchaearn: a Parish History, under Pant-teg.
9 Greenhill, Basill & Giffard, Ann: Westcountrymen in Prince Edward's Isle, p11
10 Smith, Graham: Something to Declare, p14
11 Ibid.
12 Moylon was the birthplace of Moelona, the well-known writer, who lived at New Quay for many years, the wife of the Baptist minister, the Rev Tywi Jones.
13 D Pryce Williams NLW MS 15638A

14 Schedule of CM Archives, Trevecca Group Part II NLW 3016
15 James, M E: Annibynwyr Pisgah a Phenrhiwgaled.
16 Repealed in 1814
17 An index to them is published by the Society of Genealogists: Trinity House Petitions, 1987.For further details of local petitions see S C Passmore, Some Unusual Sources, The Trinity House Petitions.
18 NLW MS 15638A
19 Nanteos MSS: see also Jones D J V: Distress and Discontent in Cardiganshire, 1814-1819.

Chapter II

1 Jones, David Lewis: Aberaeron, the Community and Seafaring 1800-1900.
2 NLW MS 10958E
3 National Archives CRES 29
4 1837, p364

Chapter III

1 p51
2 Vol I pp123-5
3 Campbell-Jones, S: Shipbuilding in New Quay 1779-1878, also Welsh Sail
4 Morfa Gwyn papers; please note though a lower figure given in 3, this is the correct cost of building the Catherine.
5 Ibid.
6 Noel Davies, op cit, for further details of this family; also Jenkins, J G: Maritime Heritage, pp28-34
7 See 3 op cit for further details
8 Davies, E B: Guide to New Quay.

9 The National Maritime Museum has a photograph of the Clarita.

10 Information from the Registers of Shipping, CRO Aberystwyth.

Chapter IV

1 Passmore, S C: New Quay at the time of the 1851 Census.

2 March, Edgar: Inshore Craft of Britain in the Days of Sail and Oar, p176

3 Passmore, ibid.

4 See also Passmore: Llanina & Cytblwyf, for more of John Jones' history under Hafod

5 Llannarth Vestry Book, NLW

6 Jenkins, J G: The Welsh Wool Industry, p55

7 Passmore, S C: Llanllwchaearn parish in the mid-19th Century.

8 Information from the late Mrs George Evans, Maen-y-groes.

9 Jenkins, ibid. p81

10 pp 7 and 8.

11 Tibbott, S Minwel: Welsh Fare.

12 Jones, E Vernon: The Footprints of a Master Craftsman, p23

13 CRO Aberystwyth D/AL Box 12 Sub-ref 29

14 In the hands of his descendants

15 NLW

16 My Street of Memories, Cambrian News 1957

17 Welsh Gazette, 1932

18 Lewis W J: Lead Mining in Wales, mentions a mine called Wheal Neptune at New Quay, but this may arise from a confused oral story as there is no evidence before 1844.

19 Atgofion Ruth Mynachlog has been translated: see Dyfed FHS
20 See the Museum's guidebook for further information
21 Evan Evans' Will DFHS 2011
22 List of Dyfed Photographers published by the Royal Photographic Society and printed in DFHS
23 For more details of the Court Records see Passmore: Llanllwchaearn: a Parish History

Chapter V

1 James, M E: op cit.
2 Passmore, S C: The Rev John Pugh, Motygido, Llannarth (1690-1763) and his School.
3 Jones, F E Llewellyn: Notes on the Jenkins Family of Dyffryn Bern.
4 Morgan, G: Circulating Schools
5 Williams, David: The Census of Religious Worship in Cardiganshire in 1851, p113
6 See The Welsh Periodical Press 1735-1900 National Library of Wales
7 Ar Fanc Sion Cwilt, pp50-57
8 Personal recollections, Dr Harry Jones
9 Williams, op cit p122
10 Ibid
11 Rees, Thomas, and Thomas, John: Hanes Eglwysi Annibynnol Cymru, Vol IV
12 James, op cit
13 In Atgofion Ruth Mynachlog Ruth recalls that her aunt was married to one of the ship's carpenters in New Quay and, when the industry declined there, the family moved to Liverpool
14 The main source of this information is Plant y Goedwig by Moelona

15 The song speaks of singing to the bells which toll the knell of the Tory candidate.
16 3 April 1932 Welsh Gazette
17 Gwynedd Jones, Ieuan: Cardiganshire Politics in the mid 19th century, p31
18 Oral tradition

Chapter VI

1 McKee, Alexander: The Golden Wreck
2 Bennett, Tom: Welsh Shipwrecks, Vol I
3 Ibid.
4 Ibid.
5 Ibid.
6 For the more recent history of the New Quay Lifeboats, see Jeff Morris' booklet sold in aid of the RNLI.
7 NLW Cilgwyn MSS
8 Campbell-Jones, S: Shipbuilding at New Quay, Appendix.
9. Westcountrymen, op cit pp165 and 255
10 Private collection
11 Passmore, Sue: Llanllwchaearn: a parish history, under Coybal
12 Jenkins, J G: Maritime Heritage, p34
13 Captain David Thomas, Rhiw-wig, born in 1867, recalled to the author how his mother had sent him to Cei Bach with 40 gold sovereigns to pay for a 1 oz share in the Nymph. She had sewn up his pockets to ensure safe delivery.
14 Shipbuilding at New Quay: Appendix.

Chapter VII

1 Welsh Sail op cit

2 Jenkins, J Geraint, and Jenkins, D: Cardiff Shipowners and Passmore, S C: The Owens of Penparc & Foel.

3 For the Anglo-Russian Grain Trade see Susan Fairlie articles, Maritime History, Vol I, No 2, Vol 2, No 1.

4 Jeffreys, Captain D E: Maritime Memories of Cardiff, p51

5 A barquentine is three-masted, square-rigged on the foremast, fore-and-aft rigged on the main and mizzen.

6 Shipbuilding in New Quay, opcit

7 Welsh Sail includes the story of an epic voyage in the Harry, the first time it was ever printed, taken from the original typescript by Phil Evans.

8 The Last of the Windjammers.

9 Private collection.

10 Morfa Gwyn papers

11 Log and Crew Agreements CRO Aberystwyth

12 A painting of the Hagar appears on the cover of Welsh Sail.

13 Photograph at the National Maritime Museum

14 Information from Mr Lewis Davies's grandson, Mr Emlyn Davies

15 The China Clippers, p227

16 Memorial University, Newfoundland

17 p117

18 i.e. her softwood timbers had been soaked in brine to give them a longer life - the average life expectancy of a softwood vessel was twenty years.

19 Lloyds Loss Book 519

20 Private Collection

21 *The War with Cape Horn* pp257-259
22 Ibid
23 Ibid
24 Davies, J Ifor: *Growing Up Among Sailors*, p45
25 See *Welsh Sail* for the strange fate of the *Resolven*, New Quay's "*Marie-Celeste*".
26 *The War with Cape Horn*, p102
27 The late Mr Hugill most kindly answered my queries about the *Doune Castle* which had not appeared in his collection.

Chapter VIII

1 From Alfred, Lord Tennyson: *The Passing of Arthur*.
2 Craig, Robin S: *Hetty Ellen of Aberystwyth and Dr Livingstone*, *Maritime Wales*, No 2, p47
3 *Shipbuilding at New Quay*, pp297-8
4 Jones, D L, op cit pp233-234
5 Ibid p212
6 *Westcountrymen* op cit p169
7 NLW NQ3589D presented by Mr John Thomas, Frondolau in 1932.
8 Roberts, Tony: *About Porthgain*
9 See *Welsh Sail* for photograph and story
10 Price, M R C: *The Lampeter, Aberaeron and New Quay Light Railway*, the Oakwood press, 1995.
11 Eifion Evans: *The Great Revival of 1904* and Adams, K and Jones, E: *A Pictorial History of the Great Revival of 1904*, (2004)
12 Thomas, Barry A: *In Search of Fossil Plants*, David Davies (Gilfach Goch)

13 Passmore, Sue: New Quay and the Great War

Epilogue

1 It is regrettable that in his otherwise admirable book Cardiganshire & the Cardis, (2010) Mike Benbough-Jackson has passed over this important era in Cardiganshire's history, simply saying Cardiganshire was too remote to make any kind of contribution to the Empire. Too little attention seems to be paid to local histories.

Bibiliography

MSS Sources

NATIONAL LIBRARY OF WALES: Parish Registers and Bishops' Transcripts for Llanllwchaearn, Llanina, Llannarth and Llandysuliogogo; the Census Records 1841-1881 for the same parishes; Diocesan Records, Churchwardens' Presentments and Vestry Records; CM Archives, Trevecca Group; Nonconformist Registers; Wills; LEA Records; Llangibby Castle Collection; R J Jones Deposit; Llanllyr; Glansevin; BRA 1940; Clement Davies Bequest; Transcript of Treasury papers NLW 16627D; Tithe Maps and Schedules of New Quay and Llannarth; New Quay Harbour Company Records; Cilgwyn Papers; Crew Agreements; unpublished Thesis: Margaret Hughes: 'Historical Geography of the Seafaring Industry of the Coast of Cardigan Bay during the 18th and 19th Centuries', MA Wales, 1962; Nanteos MSS; NLW 15638A.

NATIONAL ARCHIVES, KEW: PCC Wills, Court Rolls of the Manor of Caerwedros; Hearth Tax, Aids and Subsidies E179; Seamen's Tickets Registers; Deaths at sea; Coastguards (Admiralty Papers)

GUILDHALL, LONDON: Captains' Registers; Indexes to Lloyds' List and the Times.

NATIONAL MARITIME MUSEUM: Historic Photographs Section; Applications for Certificates.

SOCIETY OF GENEALOGISTS: Trinity House Petitions; Great Card Index.

MEMORIAL UNIVERSITY OF NEWFOUNDLAND: Crew Agreements

COUNTY RECORD OFFICE, ABERYSTWYTH: Customs Registers of Shipping; Ships' Log Books and Crew Agreements.

PRIVATE COLLECTIONS in New Quay and elsewhere.

GENERAL REFERENCE: PRINTED SOURCES

Dictionary of Welsh Biography; West Wales Historical Records, ed Francis Green; Parliamentary papers; Report of the Commissioners of Enquiry into the State of Education in Wales, 3 volumes 1847. Report on the Employment of Women and Children in Agriculture 1867.

NEWSPAPERS & PERIODICALS: Aberystwyth Observer, Baner ac Amserau Cymru, Caernarfonshire & Denbighshire Herald, Cambrian News, Cardigan & Tivy-side Advertiser, Carmarthen Historian, Carmarthen Journal, Ceredigion, Y Drysorfa, Y Diwygiwr, Y Gambo, Transactions of the Cardiganshire Antiquarian Society, Y Wasg, The Welshman, Welsh Gazette, Western Mail.

PRINTED BOOKS:

Adams, K & Jones, E:
A Pictorial history of the Revival, 1904, CWR Farnham, 2004
Bassett, T M:
The Welsh Baptists, Swansea, 1977
Bennett, Tom:
Welsh Shipwrecks, 2 volumes, Haverfordwest, 1981/82
Beynon, T:
Howell Harris's Visits to Pembrokeshire, Aberystwyth, 1966
Campbell-Jones, S:
'Shipbuilding at New Quay 1779-1878', Ceredigion, Vol VII, Nos 3 & 4, 1974-5
Welsh Sail; A photographic history of the ports of Wales, 1840-1960, Gomer Press, 1976,
4th impression, 1990. See also **Passmore, S C**
Coppack, Tom:
A Lifetime with Ships, Prescot, Lancs, 1973
Cox, J & Padfield, T:
Tracing Your Ancestors in the Public Record Office, HMSO, 1984
Craig, R S:
'Hetty Ellen of Aberystwyth and Dr Livingstone', Cymru A'r Mor/Maritime Wales, No 2, 1977
Davies, A S:
'Cardiganshire Salt Smugglers', Archaeologia Cambrensis XC1, 1936
Davies, Alun Eirug:
'Some Aspects of the Old Poor Law in Cardiganshire, 1750-1834, Ceredigion, Vol VI, No 1, 1968

David, D J:
Hanes, Hynafiaethau Ac Achyddiaeth Llanarth, Henfynyw, Llanllwchaearn a Llandyssiliogogo, Carmarthen, 1930
Davies, E Beynon:
An Early History of New Quay, Aberystwyth, 1913
Davies, Hetty Glyn:
A Village Called Llanarth, published by the author, no date, also available in Welsh: Trem Yn Ol
Davies J Ifor:
Growing Up Among Sailors, Gwynedd Archives Service, 1983
Davies, Mervyn:
The Story of Llangrannog, Cardigan, no date
Davies, Noel:
Prelude: The Red Dragon and The Rising Sun, Cowbridge, 1987
Davies, Ralph:
The Rise of the English Shipping Industry, Newton Abbot, 1972
Davies, Ronald:
Epynt Without People, Talybont, 1983
Davies, Walter:
A General View of the Agriculture and Domestic Economy of South Wales, London, 1815
De Jong, N & Moore, M E:
Launched from Prince Edward Island, PEI Heritage Foundation, 1981
Devas, Nicolette:
Two Flamboyant Fathers, London, 1966
Eames, Aled:
Ships & Seamen of Anglesey, Anglesey Antiquarian Society, 1973

Etheridge, Ken:
Welsh Costume, Ammanford, 1958
Evans, Eifion:
The Welsh Revival of 1904, Evangelical Library of Wales, Port Talbot, 1969
Evans, H T:
The Making of Modern Wales, Cardiff, no date
Evans, John:
Hanes Methodistiaeth Rhan Ddeheuol Aberteifi 1735-1900, Dolgellau, 1904
Evans, Myra:
Atgofion Ceinewydd, Aberystwyth, 1961
Fairlie, Susan:
'Shipping in the Anglo-Russian Grain Trade before 1870', Maritime History, Volume I, No 2, 1971, Vol 2, No 1, 1972
Falkus Hugh:
Master of Cape Horn, London, 1982
Ferris, Paul:
Dylan Thomas, London, 1977
Gardner, Don:
Vagabond Book of Aberaeron and New Quay, Aberystwyth, no date
Greenhill, Basil:
The Merchant Schooners, 2 volumes, Newton Abbot, 2nd edition, 1968
The Life and Death of the Merchant Sailing Ship 1815-1965, HMSO, 1980
& Giffard, Ann:
Westcountrymen in Prince Edward's Isle, Newton Abbot, 1967

Griffiths, G M:
'Glimpses of Cardiganshire in the Sessions Record', Ceredigion, Vol V, No 3, 1966
Hay, Mary:
I Saw A Ship A'Sailing, HMSO, 1981
Howard de Walden, M:
Pages From My Life, London, 1965
Howell, Dr R G:
Under Sail, Swansea Cutters, Tall Ships and Seascapes, 1830-1880, Glyn Vivian Art Gallery & Swansea City Council, 1987
Hughes, Henry:
Immortal Sails, Prescot, 1969
Hugill, Stan:
Shanties From The Seven Seas, London, 1984
Humphreys, Emyr:
The Triple Net: A Portrait of Kate Roberts, S4C, 1988
Inglis-Jones, Elizabeth:
Peacocks in Paradise, London, 1950
James, M Euronwy:
Annibynwyr Pisgah a Phenrhiwgaled, Llandysul, 1971
Jeffreys, D E:
Maritime Memories of Cardiff, Risca, 1978
Jenkins, Geraint H:
Literature, Religion & Society in Wales, 1660-1730, Cardiff, 1978
Jenkins, J Geraint:
Evan Thomas Radcliffe, a Cardiff Shipowning Company, National Museum of Wales, 1982
Maritime Heritage: The Ships and Seamen of Southern Ceredigion, Llandysul, 1982
The Welsh Woollen Industry, National Museum of Wales, 1969

'Herring Fishing in Wales', Cymru A'r Mor/Maritime Wales, No 4 1979

'Llangrannog: some aspects of the development of a coastal village' Ceredigion, Vol 3, No 3, 1958

& Jenkins, David:

Cardiff Shipowners, National Museum of Wales, 1986

Jones, D G:

Cofiant Cranogwen, Caernarfon, no date

Jones, D J V:

'Distress and Discontent in Cardiganshire, 1814-1819', Ceredigion Vol V, No 3, 1966

Jones, D Lewis:

'Aberaeron, The Community and Seafaring 1800-1900, Ceredigion, Vol VI, No 2, 1969

Jones, David:

Before Rebecca: Popular Protests in Wales, 1793-1835, London, 1973

Jones, E V:

'The Footprints of a Master Craftsman', Carmarthen Historian, Vol X, 1973

Jones, F E Llewellyn:

'The Jenkins of Dyffryn Bern', Ceredigion, Vol VI, No 2, 1969

Jones, Gareth:

The Journal of Mary Gwladys Charles, Brecon 1897-1903, published by the author, 1988

Jones, Ieuan Gwynedd:

'Cardiganshire Politics in the mid-19th century', Ceredigion, Vol V, No 1, 1964

& Jones, F E Llewellyn:

The Religious Census of 1851: South Wales, Cardiff, 1976

Jones, Ivor Wynne:
Shipwrecks of North Wales, Newton Abbot, 1973
Jones, M:
Ar Fryniau'r Glaw, Swansea, 1980
Jones, Ruth:
Atgofion Ruth Mynachlog, Llandysul, 1939. Translated by Sue Passmore, Dyfed Family History Society Journal, Vol 8, No 2-Vol 9, No 2, December 2004-April 2006
Jones, Sally:
Writers of Wales: Allen Raine, Cardiff, 1979
Jones, Capt W H S:
The Cape Horn Breed, Jarrolds, 1968
Lewis, E A:
The Welsh Port Books, Cymmrodorion Record Series No XII, London 1927
'The Port Book of Cardigan in Elizabethan and Stuart Times', Transactions of the Cardiganshire Antiquarian Society, Vols VII, IX, XI, 1931/33/35
Lewis, Samuel:
A Topographical Dictionary of Wales, London, 1840
Lloyd, Dr Lewis:
The Amity of Aberdyfi, National Library of Wales Journal, Supplement Series XIII, No 1, 1983
The Brig Susannah of Aberdyfi, published by the author, no date
The Unity of Barmouth, Gwynedd Archives, Service, 1977
Lewis, W J:
Lead Mining in Wales, Cardiff, 1967
Lowe, Jeremy:
Welsh Country Workers' Housing 1775-1875, National Museum of Wales, 1985

Lubbock, Basil:
Down Easters, Brown, Son & Ferguson Ltd, Glasgow, 1929
The Nitrate Clippers, Glasgow, 1932
The China Clippers, Glasgow, 1950
The Last of the Windjammers, 2 volumes, Glasgow, 1975
MacIntyre, Donald:
The Privateer, London, 1975
March, Edgar J:
Inshore Craft of Britain in the Days of Sail and Oar, 2 volumes Newton Abbot, 1970
Martin, Y Parch Aubrey J:
Hanes Llwynrhydowen, Llandysul, 1977
McKee, Alexander:
The Golden Wreck, New English Library, 1970
Meyrick, S R:
History of Cardiganshire, London 1907
Moelona:
Plant y Goedwig, London Missionary Society, 1921
Molloy, Pat:
And They Blessed Rebecca, Llandysul, 1982
Morgan, D W:
Brief Glory, The Brython Press, 1948
Morgan, K O:
Lloyd George Family Letters 1885-1936, University of Wales & Oxford University Press, 1973
Wales in British Politics, 1868-1922, Cardiff, 1963
Morgan, Prys:
The Eighteenth Century Renaissance, New History of Wales, Llandybie, 1981
Morris, Jeff:
The Story of New Quay (Dyfed) Lifeboats, RNLI, 1987

Morris, Lewis:
Plans of the Harbours, Bays and Roads in St George's Channel, 1748
Morris, William:
Plans of the Principal Harbours, Bays and Roads in St George's and the Bristol Channel, Shrewsbury, 1801
Moyse-Bartlett, H:
From Sail to Steam, Historical Association, 1968
National Library of Wales:
The Welsh Periodical Press, 1735-1900, 1987
Oxley, Geoffrey W:
Poor Relief in England and Wales, 1601-1834, Newton Abbot, 1974
Parry-Jones, D:
My Own Folk, Llandysul, 1972
Welsh Country Upbringing, The Ffynnon Press. 1976
Welsh Country Characters, The Ffynnon Press, 1973
Passmore, S C:
'Llanllwchaearn at the time of the 1851 Census', *Dyfed Family History Society Journal*, Vol 2, Nos 7 & 8, 1987
'New Quay at the Time of the 1851 Census', *Ceredigion*, Vol X, No 3, 1986
The Owens of Penparc & Foel: The History of a Llandysuliogogo Family,1988
'Trinity House Petitions', *DFHS Journal*, Vol 3, No 5, 1989
One Village's War, New Quay in the Second World War, 1995
New Quay and the Great War, Ceredigion Museum, 1996
'Manorial Records', *DFHS Journal*, Vol V, No 6, April 1996
'The Revd John Pugh, Motygido, Llannarth (1690-1763) and his School, *Ceredigion*, Vol XII, No 4, 1996

Translation of Atgofion Ruth Mynachlog DFHS Vol 8, No2 -Vol 9, No 2, December 2004-April 2006
Llanllwchaearn: a parish history, Guildford, 2010
Llanina & Cytblwyf, Guildford, 2011
'Dyfed Shipping Wills' and 'Dyfed Farm Wills', DFHS, Vol 10, No 8, & Vol 11, No 1, 2011
See also **Campbell-Jones, S**
Pearse, Ronald:
The Last of a Glorious Era, London, 1934
Peate, Iorwerth C:
Clock and Watch Makers of Wales, National Museum of Wales, 1960
Guide to the Collections of Welsh Byegones, National Museum of Wales, 1929
Price, M R C:
The Lampeter, Aberayron and New Quay Light Railway, Oakwood Press, 1995
Raine, Allen:
Torn Sails, Hutchinson & Co, no date
Rees, T & Thomas, J:
Hanes Eglwysi Annibynol Cymru, Cyf IV, Tyst Cymreig, Liverpool,1875
Rees, William:
An Historical Atlas of Wales from Early to Modern Times London, 1959
Roberts, Tony:
About Porthgain, Abercastle Publications, no date
Royal Photographic Society:
'Dyfed Photographers', Dyfed Family History Society Journal, Vol 3, No 6, 1990
Sarnicol (Thomas, T J):
Ar Fanc Sion Cwilt: Detholiad o Ysgrifau Sarnicol, Llandysul, 1972

Scarlett, Bernard:
Shipminder, The Story of H M Coastguard, Pelham Books, 1971
Shaw, Captain H:
Schooner Captain, Truro, 1972
Slade, W J:
Out of Appledore, Conway Maritime Press, 1972
Smith, Graham:
Something To Declare, London, 1980
Stevenson, Frances:
Lloyd George, A Diary, London, 1971
Thomas, Barry A:
In Search of Fossil Plants: David Davies (Gilfach Goch), National Museum of Wales, 1986
Thomas Caitlin & Tremlett, George:
Life with Dylan Thomas, New York, 1987
Thomas, Dylan:
Quite Early One Morning, London 1954
Collected Poems, 1934-1952, London, 1952
Thomas, Peter:
Strangers From A Secret Land, Llandysul, 1987
Tibbot, S Minwel:
Welsh Fare, Welsh Folk Museum, 1976
Villiers, Alan:
The War With Cape Horn, London, 1973
Webb, William:
Coastguard! HMSO, 1976
White, E W:
British Fishing Boats & Coastal Craft, HMSO, 1950
Wiliam, Eurwyn:
Home-Made Houses, National Museum of Wales, 1988
Melin Bompren Corn Mill, National Museum of Wales, 1977

Wilkinson, Walter:
Puppets in Wales, London, 1948
Williams, David:
'The Census of Religious Worship in Cardiganshire in 1851', Ceredigion, Vol IV No 2, 1961
Williams, D J:
The Old Farmhouse, London, 1961
Williams, R J:
Y Parch John Roberts, DD, Khasia, Lyfyrfa'r Methodistiaid Calfinaidd, Caernarfon, 1923

INDEX

B

F

I

J

L

M

O

Q

V

W

CPSIA information can be obtained at www.ICGtesting.com
Printed in the USA
BVOW072135170712

295498BV00001B/1/P

9 781781 485095